Teacher Guide
Passwords
Social Studies Vocabulary
World Geography and Cultures

Developers: Maureen Devine Sotoohi

Writer: Carol Domblewski

Cover Design: Susan Hawk

Photo Credits: Front cover: clockwise from top left: Wikipedia Commons;
©2007 JupiterImages Corporation; Courtesy of NASA;
©Ludovic Maisant/CORBIS

Reviewers: Curriculum Associates, Inc. would like to acknowledge the contribution
of the educators who reviewed *Passwords* at various stages of its development. Their
insightful comments have made our program a better one for teachers and students.

Gracie Alvear
Bilingual/ESL/Immigrant Student Service
Elementary Supervisor
Edinburg CISD
Edinburg, Texas

Jackie Baldwin
Secondary Reading Senior Coordinator
Instructional Services Division
Polk County Schools
Bartow, Florida

Lorraine Cruz
Principal
Ames Middle School
Chicago, Illinois

Leonila Izaguirre
Bilingual-ESL Director
Pharr-San Juan-Alamo ISD
Pharr, Texas

Judy Lewis
Director, State and Federal Programs
Folsom Cordova Unified School District
Folsom, California

Dominique Mongeau
Categorical Program Adviser
Carson Street Elementary School
Los Angeles Unified School District
Carson, California

CURRICULUM ASSOCIATES®, INC.

Table of Contents

ISBN 978-0-7609-4505-6

©2008—Curriculum Associates, Inc.
North Billerica, MA 01862
15 14 13 12 11 10 9 8 7 6 5 4 3 2 1

Passwords: Social Studies Vocabulary is designed to build the vocabulary essential to understanding the key concepts students are studying in social studies. The topic areas and vocabulary words used in ***Passwords: Social Studies Vocabulary*** have been chosen based on the social studies standards developed by individual states. The topics and vocabulary words also align with the basal social studies textbooks of major publishers.

Passwords: Social Studies Vocabulary is recommended for all students who need practice with the vocabulary that will help them succeed in social studies. These students may include English language learners as well as other striving learners. See pages 9–11 of this teacher guide for vocabulary teaching strategies that will help teachers meet the needs of all their students.

The lessons in ***Passwords: Social Studies Vocabulary*** are grouped by topic area, and each lesson may be taught independently. Teachers may choose to go through the book lesson by lesson. Alternatively, they may select individual lessons that correspond to the topic being taught in class. By providing an overview of grade-appropriate topics, ***Passwords: Social Studies Vocabulary*** may also be used to help students prepare and review for standardized tests in social studies.

The ***Passwords: Social Studies Vocabulary*** student book reading selections are available on an audio CD. The CD is a useful tool to use with English language learners or other students who would benefit from listening to the reading selection multiple times. Auditory learners will find listening to the selections on the CD especially helpful.

Use this product
right away, the right way!
e-Training for Teachers
CAtraining.com

Passwords: Social Studies Vocabulary student books have been written and designed to provide students with a text that is "considerate," or reader friendly. Three hallmarks of considerate text are: clear text structure, coherent writing, and audience appropriateness. *Passwords: Social Studies Vocabulary* incorporates these characteristics of considerate text into every lesson.

Text Structure

The reading selections in *Passwords: Social Studies Vocabulary* feature text structures that exhibit clear organizational patterns. In descriptive text, information is given in a logical order of importance. For sequential text, events are presented in the order in which they occur. In cause-and-effect text, the relation between the actions or events is clearly stated.

Coherent Writing

The social studies concepts and ideas presented in *Passwords: Social Studies Vocabulary* are clearly stated. An introductory paragraph states the topic of the lesson. All the information in the reading selection connects to the topic. No extraneous material confuses readers. Headings and subheads highlight the cohesion of each text segment. Transitional words and phrases signal the relation between actions or concepts.

Audience Appropriateness

Although the readability of *Passwords: Social Studies Vocabulary* reading selections is below grade level, the concepts and material in the selections are grade appropriate. Prereading activities activate students' prior knowledge. Activities that follow the reading selection help teachers evaluate student understanding.

Look for these signs of considerate text in the *Passwords: Social Studies Vocabulary* student books.

- Short line length for increased readability
- Simple sentence structure
- Paragraphs with clear topic sentences and relevant supporting details
- Introductory subheads
- Vocabulary words boldfaced in text
- Definitions of vocabulary words near the first use of the word
- Simple font
- Clean page layout
- Appropriate, not overwhelming, visuals
- Illustrations support content

The student book for *World Geography and Cultures* has 15 lessons.

Features of the Lesson

Each lesson of the student book contains these features:
- Target Vocabulary
- Lesson Opener
- Reading Selection
- Graphics
- Activities A–D
- Word Root
- Write!

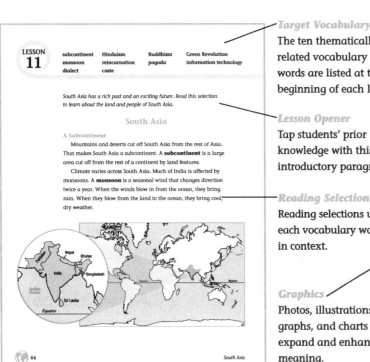

Target Vocabulary
The ten thematically related vocabulary words are listed at the beginning of each lesson.

Lesson Opener
Tap students' prior knowledge with this introductory paragraph.

Reading Selection
Reading selections use each vocabulary word in context.

Graphics
Photos, illustrations, graphs, and charts expand and enhance meaning.

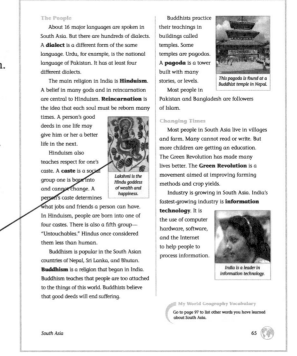

Progressively difficult activities follow each reading selection.

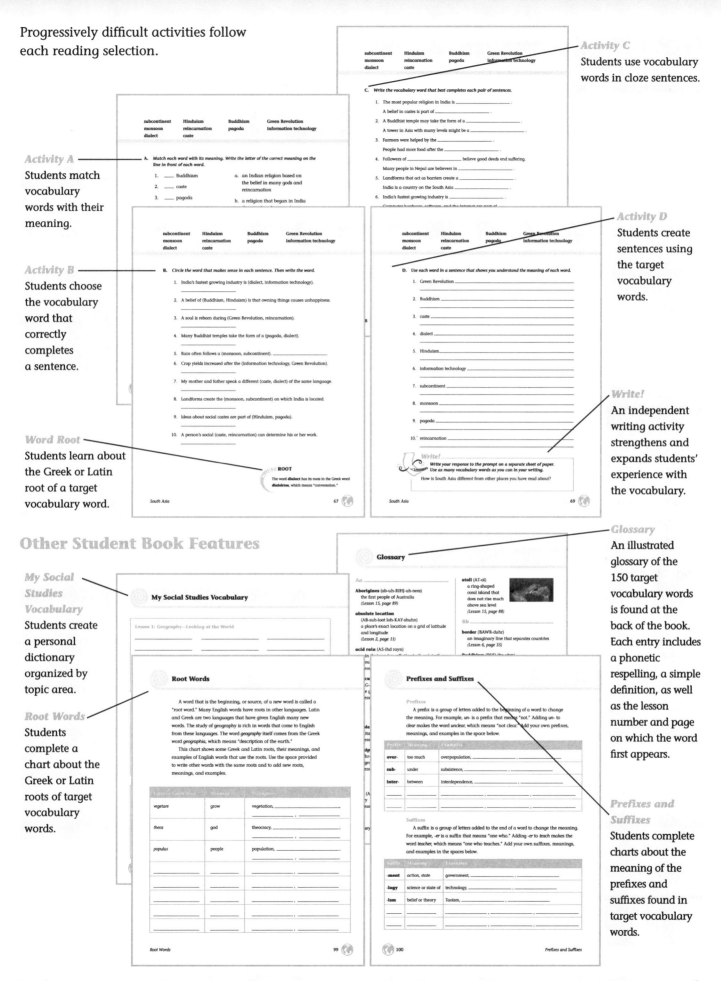

Activity A
Students match vocabulary words with their meaning.

Activity B
Students choose the vocabulary word that correctly completes a sentence.

Word Root
Students learn about the Greek or Latin root of a target vocabulary word.

Activity C
Students use vocabulary words in cloze sentences.

Activity D
Students create sentences using the target vocabulary words.

Write!
An independent writing activity strengthens and expands students' experience with the vocabulary.

Other Student Book Features

My Social Studies Vocabulary
Students create a personal dictionary organized by topic area.

Root Words
Students complete a chart about the Greek or Latin roots of target vocabulary words.

Glossary
An illustrated glossary of the 150 target vocabulary words is found at the back of the book. Each entry includes a phonetic respelling, a simple definition, as well as the lesson number and page on which the word first appears.

Prefixes and Suffixes
Students complete charts about the meaning of the prefixes and suffixes found in target vocabulary words.

The Teacher Guide for *Passwords: Social Studies Vocabulary* contains resources that may be used to introduce, support, and extend students' vocabulary studies. The Teacher Guide includes guided instruction for each student book lesson.

Multi-Step Lesson Plan

Passwords: Social Studies Vocabulary is built upon the premise that students benefit most from the direct instruction of vocabulary. Each lesson as presented in the Teacher Guide follows a multi-step lesson plan.

1. Introduction of the target vocabulary
2. Activation of students' prior knowledge
3. Provision of the meaning of unknown words
4. Creation by students of visual representations using graphic organizers
5. Further experiences with the target vocabulary
6. Activities that help students retain the word and its meaning

Listening, Speaking, Reading, and Writing

Passwords: Social Studies Vocabulary provides opportunities for students to practice the target vocabulary words while listening, speaking, reading, and writing. These icons indicate opportunities for students to use the vocabulary words in different domains.

 Listening

 Speaking

 Reading

 Writing

Features of the Guided Teaching Lessons

Each lesson of the Teacher Guide contains these features:

- Target Vocabulary with definitions
- Cognates
- Vocabulary Strategy
- Lesson Summary
- Before Reading
- Word and Definition Cards
- Reproduced student book pages
- During Reading
- After Reading
- Annotated student book activity pages
- Extensions
- Ideas for introducing the Write! activity
- Sample answer for Write!
- Word Root extension

Target Vocabulary
The ten target vocabulary words are listed here with convenient, student-friendly definitions.

Cognates
Cognates can be a powerful tool in developing the vocabulary of English language learners.

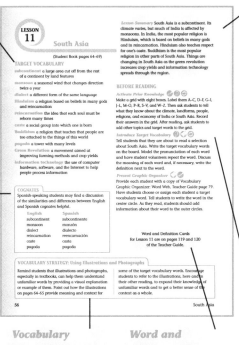

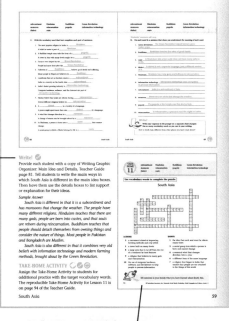

Lesson Summary
Use the summary for a quick introduction to the topic of the lesson.

Reproduced Student Book Pages
Student book lessons are reproduced for easy reference.

Before Reading
Questions and activities activate students' prior knowledge, build background, and motivate students to read. Graphic organizers are provided to build students' understanding of the target vocabulary.

Vocabulary Strategy
A vocabulary strategy that is particularly appropriate for the lesson is highlighted here.

Word and Definition Cards
Teacher Guide page references make it easy to find and use the word and definition cards.

During Reading
Includes suggestions for presenting the reading selection and tips for explaining possibly difficult or confusing vocabulary words.

After Reading
Provides guidance in using the graphic organizers to sum up the lesson and reminders to direct students to My Social Studies Vocabulary and the Glossary.

Activities
The reproduced student book activity pages are annotated.

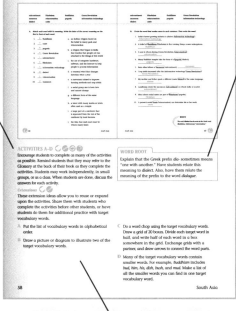

Word Root
Provides additional information about the student book Word Root.

Write!
Each guided lesson provides hints about presenting the Write! activity as well as a sample answer.

Extensions
An extension idea for each student book activity allows the activities to be reused or expanded.

Take-Home Activity
The Take-Home Activity for the lesson is reproduced with the answers provided.

Other Teacher Guide Features

- **Vocabulary Teaching Strategies**
  Information and tips about how to employ vocabulary teaching strategies that have proven effective with struggling learners and English language learners begin on page 9.

- **Research Summary**
  A summary of the research that forms the basis of **Passwords: Social Studies Vocabulary** is on pages 12–15.

- **Reproducibles**
  Pages 76–128 of the Teacher Guide contain reproducibles for you to share with students.

  ### Graphic Organizers
  You may either photocopy the graphic organizers for students to use or use the sample graphic organizer as a model for students to create their own. The Before Reading section of each guided lesson suggests a particular vocabulary graphic organizer to use with the lesson. The Write! section of each guided lesson suggests a writing graphic organizer to use with the Write! activity.

  - **Vocabulary Graphic Organizers**

    Word Wheel   Students write the target vocabulary word in the center circle. They then add information about the word on the outer lines, or spokes. Students may use the lines to write antonyms, synonyms, prefixes, suffixes, a definition, or examples.

    What Is it Like?   Students write a target vocabulary word in the center box and then fill in the outer boxes with a synonym, an antonym, an example of the word, and an example of what the word is not.

    Vocabulary Map   Students write a target vocabulary word in the center box. They then add information about the target vocabulary word in the outer boxes. This information includes a definition, a synonym, and an antonym. Students also draw a picture illustrating the word and write a sentence using the word.

Word Web   Students write the targeted word or topic in the central circle. They then add information about the word or topic in the outer circles. Students may use the outer circles to write antonyms, synonyms, prefixes, suffixes, a definition, or examples.

- **Writing Graphic Organizers**

  Cause-and-Effect Chart   Use this chart when the Write! activity asks students to write about cause and effect. Students write causes in one set of boxes and effects in a corresponding set of boxes.

  Main Idea and Details Chart   This graphic organizer may be used with a variety of writing tasks. Students write a main idea in one box and the details that support it in another box.

  Two-Column Chart   This graphic organizer can be used with a variety of writing tasks. Students could use the chart to write a main idea in one column and the details that support it in the other column. They may also use the chart's columns to compare and contrast two things, to list problems and solutions, or causes and effects.

Topic Web   A web may be used with a variety of types of writing. Generally, students write the topic, or main idea, of their writing in the center circle and important points or supporting details in the outer circles.

Word and Definition Cards
Word cards for each target vocabulary word as well as cards with the definitions for the words are on pages 99–128 of this Teacher Guide. You may either cut the cards out of the book or photocopy them, cut them apart, and then use them. For ideas on how to use the word and definition cards, see page 10 of this Teacher Guide.

Take-Home Activities
Each student book lesson has a take-home activity for additional practice and an opportunity for students to share what they have learned with family members.

Vocabulary Teaching Strategies

These teaching strategies have been shown to be effective with English language learners, but all students who are studying vocabulary will find them helpful.

Accessing Prior Knowledge

Like their English-speaking peers, English language learners come to the classroom with a large body of knowledge. The challenge as a teacher of English language learners is tapping into this knowledge. Before introducing a lesson topic, ask students what they already know about the subject. By doing this, you not only acknowledge students' experiences, but you also find out what information and misinformation students have about the topic. This will enable you to plan a more relevant and focused lesson. Each student book lesson of **Passwords: Social Studies Vocabulary** begins with an introductory paragraph written to tap into students' prior knowledge and to provide motivation for reading. In addition, this Teacher Guide includes a prior knowledge activity for each lesson.

Picture File

Use magazines or Web sources to create a file of pictures for each social studies topic. Students will enjoy looking for pictures and pasting them to construction paper. Use the pictures to illustrate target vocabulary words or key concepts. Pictures can be used before, during, or after reading in matching games, gallery walks, and as writing prompts.

Graphic Organizers

This Teacher Guide includes four vocabulary graphic organizers and four writing graphic organizers that can be reproduced for use by students. (See pages 76–83.)

Vocabulary graphic organizers can provide students with a visual representation of a word's meaning by showing examples, synonyms, drawings, descriptions, or the definition of the word. Students can add to the graphic organizer as their understanding of the word increases.

Writing graphic organizers help students organize their thoughts and plan their writing. The writing graphic organizers included in this Teacher Guide are intended for use with different kinds of Write! activities.

Total Physical Response

Total Physical Response, or TPR, is a language-teaching method first developed by Dr. James Asher, a professor of psychology. Asher based his method on his observations of how children learn their native language. In TPR, teachers replace parents, modeling verbal commands, while students respond physically. As a language-teaching method, TPR emphasizes listening and physical response over written language. It has been found to be an effective method for teaching vocabulary. In using TPR to teach vocabulary, teachers and students use movement to associate a word with its meaning. For example, to teach the target vocabulary word *channel*, have your students get up and form two lines that are parallel. Have one student walk between the two lines. To use TPR in your classroom, give commands that require a physical response from students. When they are ready, students can reverse roles, giving commands to you and to fellow students.

Context Clues

Students need to be directly instructed on how to use context clues to help them figure out the meaning of unknown words. There are several different kinds of context clues.

- **Definition**
  In this type of context clue, a definition, or restatement, of the unknown word is provided in the text. Words that signal a definition context clue include *means, refers to,* or *is.* Definition context clues are frequently used in **Passwords: Social Studies Vocabulary**.

- **Synonym**
  Writers sometimes use familiar words with similar meanings to build meaning for an unknown or unfamiliar word.

- **Example**
  Point out to students that writers will sometimes provide an example that will help them figure out the meaning of an unfamiliar word. Words that may signal an example include *like, these, for example,* and *such as.*

Cognates

Cognates are words in different languages that resemble one another in both sound and meaning. Spanish and English have many cognates, especially in the area of social studies where words in both languages draw upon Latin and Greek roots. Some cognates are spelled identically, although pronunciation differs; for example the words *arable, rural,* and *oasis.* Others are spelled similarly; *tribe* and *tribu.* Other words that seem similar are not cognates at all. *Bigote* does not mean "bigot"; it means "mustache."

Teachers cannot assume that Spanish-speaking students will automatically or correctly connect an English word with a Spanish cognate. To help students develop the ability to recognize cognates, each ***Passwords: Social Studies Vocabulary*** Teacher Guide lesson includes a list of the Spanish cognates for the target vocabulary in that lesson. As you discuss these cognates with students, point out spelling patterns, such as *-tion* (English) and *-ción* (Spanish). This will help students develop generalizations about language patterns and enhance their ability to use their knowledge of their native language to learn English. Encourage your Spanish-speaking students to guess at the meaning of words in English based on their knowledge of Spanish. If you read the selections aloud, ask Spanish speakers to indicate when they think they hear a cognate. If students read the selections themselves, have them write down the words they think might be cognates. Discuss possible cognates when students have finished reading the selection. Write the word pairs on the board and have students come to the board and circle the similarities between the two words. Have students look for patterns. Students who speak languages other than Spanish may also be able to find English cognates of words from their native languages.

Greek and Latin Roots

Introducing the study of Greek and Latin roots to students who are learning English may initially seem to be adding another layer of difficulty to language learning. However, students who speak a Romance language (Spanish, French, Italian, Portuguese, Romanian) will often find that the Latin or Greek root of an English word is similar to a word they know in their own language. Students who speak Haitian Creole may find that their native language, which draws heavily upon French, also has many links to Latin.

When teaching students how to use roots to determine word meaning, remind them that many long English words are made up of smaller parts. The root of the word is the part that contains the most important aspect of the word's meaning. For example, if students come across the word *theocracy* and they recognize the root *theo* from their study of Greek and Latin roots and they remember that the root *theo* is related to "god," they can begin to figure out that *theocracy* has something to do with religion.

Students will find a chart of Greek and Latin roots, with examples of target vocabulary words that have those roots, on page 99 of the student book.

Prefixes and Suffixes

A prefix is a word part that is attached to the beginning of a base word. A suffix is a word part that is attached to the end of a base word. The meaning of a prefix or suffix combines with the meaning of the base word. For example, the prefix *ex-*, meaning "out," combines with *port* to form *export*, a good that is sent out of a country. The suffix *-ism,* meaning "state or theory of," combines with *national* to form *nationalism*. Knowing the meaning of common prefixes and suffixes is another tool students can use to help them figure out the meaning of unknown words and remember the meaning of words they are learning.

Students will find a chart of common prefixes and suffixes, with examples of target vocabulary words that have these prefixes or suffixes, on page 100 of the student book.

Word Cards

This Teacher Guide includes reproducible word and definition cards on pages 99–128. Each page contains one lesson's words or definitions. These cards can be used in teacher-led activities, and small group activities, to introduce new vocabulary, and to review vocabulary and concepts. Word cards are helpful to visual, kinesthetic, and aural learners. Word cards provide students with visual cues and constant reinforcement. Many word card activities require you to create copies of the cards. You can photocopy the cards on cardstock or on plain paper. If you want to use the cards as flashcards, with the definition on the back, photocopy the pages as two-sided copies. For many activities, however, you will need cards with one blank side and the word or the definition on the other side. After you make the copies, cut the cards apart. Store the cards in labeled plastic zipper bags for easy access. If you want to provide each student with a set of cards, you might consider having students create their own cards using blank 3½ × 5 file cards. Although you will certainly come up with many ideas of how to use these cards on your own, here are a few activities to begin with.

- **Word Wall**

  A Word Wall can be a great tool in helping students learn vocabulary. Although words are generally displayed on a bulletin board, you can also use more portable display surfaces, such as a shower curtain or a trifold board. Add words to the Word Wall as you introduce the target vocabulary. Review the words daily. Change the words as you begin a new lesson. Word Walls lend themselves to a variety of activities.

  ### Five Clues

  Have each student number their paper from one to five. Give a clue about one of the words on the Word Wall. Students should write down the word they think you are thinking of. Keep giving clues (up to five) until everyone has guessed the word you were thinking of.

  ### Lights On!

  You'll need a flashlight for this activity. Turn off the classroom lights. Then point the flashlight at one word on the Word Wall. Call on a student to read the word and either use it in a sentence or provide the definition. When the student is successful, it is his or her turn to point the flashlight at a word and choose another student to read the word.

  ### Wordo

  Provide each student with a bingo-type grid with six blank spaces. Tell students to fill in the blanks with words from the Word Wall. Put the corresponding definition cards into a jar. Pull the definition cards from the jar one by one. Read the definition and have students cover the corresponding word on their grid with a marker. When the entire card is covered, Wordo!

- **Card Games**

  The word cards can be used in many different card games, some of which are variations of games played with regular playing cards. Here are a few ideas for games using the word cards.

  ### Concentration

  The object of this game is to find matching pairs. Prepare two sets of cards. One set of cards has the vocabulary words and the other set has the definitions. Prepare from 10 cards (for 5 matches) to 30 cards (15 matches). Mix up the two sets of cards. Place the cards face down in rows. Players take turns turning over pairs of cards. If the cards match, the player makes a sentence using the vocabulary word. If the cards don't match, play goes to the next player. If the student successfully creates a sentence using the vocabulary word, he or she goes again. The player with the most cards at the end is the winner.

  ### Guess the Word

  This game is for four students, playing in pairs. Prepare a card for each vocabulary word. Put the cards face down in the middle of the table. The first student of the first pair picks a card and gives a one-word clue to his or her partner that will enable the partner to guess the target vocabulary word. If the partner does not guess the word, the word goes to a member of the other pair who gives a hint to his or her partner. The team that successfully guesses the word keeps the card. The team with the most cards wins.

What Is the Need for *Passwords: Social Studies Vocabulary*?

Learning academic vocabulary is essential to each student's comprehension of content-area materials. Researchers (Bailey, 2007; Resnick, 2006; Ogle, Klemp, & McBride, 2007; Yarbrough, 2007) have shown that many content-area texts may present learning barriers to students. In a 2006 textbook survey by Education Market Research, teachers were asked about the biggest problems they experienced with their current text. Teachers stated that texts that are "hard for students to read" (35.2%) was the biggest problem, followed closely by "doesn't meet needs of diverse students" (31.4%). Several factors may make a text hard to read, such as:

- A textbook analysis found that some texts are written approximately 2 to 4 reading levels above grade level. This fact highlights why students may struggle with content-area instructional materials (Yarbrough, 2007).

- Social studies texts are more lexically dense and the wording of these texts are not typical to what students hear and say in everyday life (Bailey, 2007).

- Background knowledge of a topic may not be incorporated into a new lesson, causing a disconnect for students who are not familiar with a specific social-studies topic (Ogle, Klemp, & McBride, 2007).

- Struggling readers have difficulty with nonlinear reading. Excess use of photographs, charts, maps, and graphs can inhibit rather than support a struggling reader's comprehension (Ogle, Klemp, & McBride, 2007).

Concerns about students' comprehension of content-area texts continues to grow. The 2006 National Assessment of Educational Progress (NAEP) Social Studies Assessment reported minor increases in the "Basic" level of performance of 4th- and 8th-grade students (Lee & Weiss, 2007). While these results are encouraging, the reauthorization of the No Child Left Behind Act (NCLB) proposes to make NAEP results even more significant. Under the NCLB reauthorization, NAEP assessment scores will be listed alongside each state's scores. This comparison of scores is meant to close the achievement gap between state tests and the NAEP tests (U.S. Department of Ed., 2007). This new initiative heightens the need for students to master academic vocabulary for better comprehension of content-area materials.

Passwords: Social Studies Vocabulary is a tool that can support students who struggle with "hard-to-read" texts. It unites students with a singular goal of successfully learning the academic language of social studies. This goal is attainable through the instructional features and strategies that research has proven to be effective with diverse student populations.

Why Is *Passwords: Social Studies Vocabulary* Helpful to ELL Students?

Academic language proficiency is the ability of the student to comprehend, speak, read, and write when the context is reduced and the topic is cognitively demanding. Examples of cognitively demanding activities are reading textbooks, writing long compositions, learning new concepts, and mastering local and state requirements that test students on the academic language of each content area. Zelasko & Antunez (2000) state that "without mastery of classroom English, they [ELL students] will have difficulty competing academically in an all-English setting." The importance of learning academic language is confirmed by additional researchers (August, Carlo, Dressler, & Snow, 2005):

- "Vocabulary development is one of the greatest challenges to reading instruction for ELLs, because in order to read fluently and comprehend what is written, students need to use not just phonics, but context" (Antunez, 2002).

- "For English language learners, academic English is like a third language, their second language being the social English of the hallways, community, and media. And whereas students are exposed to social English in various settings, academic language acquisition is generally limited to the classroom. . . . Many English language learners, even those with well-developed social language, struggle to master the complex language of school" (Zwiers, 2004/2005).

What Are the Strategies and Features in *Passwords: Social Studies Vocabulary* that Research Has Proven to Be Effective with ELL Students?

Social studies is a cognitively demanding school subject. In addition, the vocabulary of social studies is also considered as Tier III vocabulary, which requires direct and explicit instruction (Beck, McKeown, & Kucan, 2002). This is especially important for ELL students. The first step to comprehending the content of a school subject is to understand the vocabulary and language of the school subject. ***Passwords: Social Studies Vocabulary*** incorporates ELL instructional recommendations from content-area experts for teaching vocabulary.

Marzano & Pickering (2005), in *Building Academic Vocabulary*, promote a six-step process for teaching new terms. This process is also integrated in ***Passwords: Social Studies Vocabulary***.

Step 1: Provide a description, an explanation, or an example of the new term (along with a nonlinguistic representation).

Step 2: Ask students to restate the description, explanation, or example in their own words.

Step 3: Ask students to construct a picture, symbol, or graphic representing the term.

Step 4: Engage students periodically in activities that help them add to their knowledge of the terms.

Step 5: Engage students periodically to discuss the terms with one another.

Step 6: Involve students periodically in games that allow them to play with terms.

Additionally, educational experts and researchers from numerous professional organizations (Association for Supervision and Curriculum Developers, English Language Summit, and International Reading Association) have created a list of instructional recommendations that have been found to be effective, especially with ELL students. While these organizations are separate entities, they share some common recommendations. These recommendations are integrated throughout ***Passwords: Social Studies Vocabulary***.

Passwords: Social Studies Vocabulary Uses . . .	**Research Says . . .**
Direct Instruction Within Context (SB, Reading Passage & Activities A–D)	*"The teaching of individual words is most effective when learners are given both definitional and contextual information, when learners actively process the new word meanings, and when they experience multiple encounters with words"* (Graves & Watts-Taffe, 2002).
Prior-Knowledge Activation (SB, Prereading Activity; TG)	*"To facilitate communication of content knowledge, teachers can offer support in several ways: Plan adequate time to activate students' prior knowledge and encourage students to share what they already know in journals, small groups, or paired brainstorming sessions"* (Rolón, 2002/2003).
Collaborative Learning (SB, Prereading Activity & Activities A–D; TG)	*"Students interacting verbally with other native speakers of English pick up vocabulary and content knowledge"* (Association of American Publishers, 2004). *"Research and common sense . . . confirm that interacting with other people about what we are learning deepens the understanding of everyone involved—particularly when we are learning new terms"* (Marzano & Pickering, 2005).
Differentiated Instruction (SB, Activities A–D; TG)	*"Numerous theorists and contemporary translators of brain research propose that students do not learn effectively when tasks are too simple or too complex for their particular readiness levels. Rather, say these researchers, tasks must be moderately challenging for the individual for growth to occur"* (Tomlinson, 2004).
Parental Engagement (TG, Take-Home Activities)	*"The evidence is consistent, positive, and convincing: families have a major influence on their children's achievement in school and through life"* (Henderson & Mapp, 2002).
Total Physical Response (TG, Vocabulary Teaching Strategies section, During Reading Activity)	*"Having children physically act out songs, poems, or readings—all forms of TPR methodology—is an effective way to support vocabulary development"* (Drucker, 2003). *In a research synthesis, Slavin & Cheung (2005) state that teachers of English language learners may use language development strategies, such as total physical response, to help students internalize new vocabulary.*

(Continues)

(Continued)

Passwords: Social Studies Vocabulary Uses . . .	**Research Says . . .**
Considerate Text (SB, Reading Passages)	*"Certain features of text make it more 'considerate,' or easier to read and understand. The features should have clear concepts, consistent text structure, references that are easy to locate, and vocabulary that is precise and relates clearly to the subject. . . . A considerate text makes comprehension easier" (Dyck & Pemberton, 2002).*
Graphic Organizers (Semantic Feature Analysis & Semantic Mapping) (TG, Pre- & Post-reading Activities)	*Hedrick, Harmon, & Linerode (2004, 2000) have analyzed content-area textbooks and have concluded that "textbooks infrequently include visual representations of concepts as a vocabulary instructional strategy."*
Clear and Explicit Illustrations and Artwork (SB, Reading Passages)	*"Giving an ESL student a nonlinguistic representation will provide a way for them to understand the meaning of the term that is not dependent on an understanding of English" (Marzano & Pickering, 2005).*
Deep Word-Study Activities (Roots, Prefixes, Suffixes, Cognates) (SB/TG)	*Students may find learning English easier if there are similar roots and pre/suffixes between their first language and English. Hansen (2006) suggests exploring cognates in order to aid students in making connections between their first language and English.* *"Teaching a word's facets of meaning moves students beyond a narrow definition of a word" (Beck, McKeown, & Kucan, 2002).*
Word Play Activities (TG, Take-Home Activities, Word Cards)	*Researchers (Marzano & Pickering, 2005; Paynter, Bodrova, & Doty, 2005; Richek, 2005) stress that word play builds a strong connection to newly learned vocabulary.* *"Activities using words in games, connecting words, and manipulating words creatively result in excellent student learning" (Beck, McKeown, & Kucan, 2002).*
Association/ Connection Methods: (Personal Connection, Picture Connection, Word Connection) (SB/TG, throughout each lesson, Glossary)	*"This step is particularly important to ESL students. Whereas they might be constrained in their ability to devise a linguistic description, explanation, or example, they will not be constrained in their ability to create a nonlinguistic representation . . . These representations will most likely reflect the students' native culture, which is exactly the intent. Learning academic terms involves making connections with things familiar to us, and these things commonly arise from experiences native to our culture" (Marzano & Pickering, 2005).*
Modeling Through Audio (*Passwords* Audio CD)	*"When English language learners can simultaneously hear and read content-related information . . . it helps them decipher the text structures commonly found in textbooks" (Rubinstein-Ávila, 2006).*
Read Alouds (TG)	*"Teacher read-alouds are perhaps the most consistent activity used by classroom teachers that provides frequent, if not daily, opportunities to enhance the literacy of ELLs by integrating effective vocabulary development practices" (Hickman, Pollard-Durodola, & Vaughn, 2004).*
Speaking, Listening, Reading, Writing Experiences (SB/TG, throughout each lesson)	*"Successful word learning is active. Students learn words by using them. Thinking, saying, and writing new words help us make new words our own" (Bromley, 2003).* *García (1999) recommended that teachers use ". . . curriculum materials that are rich in opportunities for speaking, listening, reading, and writing in English."*

References

Antunez, B. (2002). English language learners and the five essential components of reading comprehension. Accessed February 27, 2006, from http://www.readingrockets.org/articles/341#vocab.

Association of American Publishers. (Fall 2004). English Language Learners summit proceedings, AAP School Division. Summit on English Language Learners. The Washington Court Hotel, Washington, DC. October 12, 2004. Accessed January 16, 2006, from http://www.publishers.org/SchoolDiv/research/research_03/research_03_Rep_05.htm.

August, D., Carlo, M., Dressler, C., & Snow, C. (2005). The critical role of vocabulary development for English language learners. *Learning Disabilities Research & Practice, 20*(1), 50–57.

Bailey, A. L. (Ed.). (2007). *The language demands of school: Putting academic English to the test.* New Haven: Yale University Press.

Beck, I. L., McKeown, M. G., & Kucan, L. (2002). *Bringing words to life: Robust vocabulary instruction.* New York: Guilford Press.

Bromley, K. (2003, April). Vocabulary S-t-r-e-t-c-h-e-r-s, *Instructor, 112*(7).

Drucker, M. J. (2003). What reading teachers should know about ESL learners: Good teaching is teaching for all. *The Reading Teacher, 57*(1).

Dyck, N., & Pemberton, J. B. (2002). A model for making decisions about text adaptations. *Intervention in School & Clinic, 38*(1).

García, E. (1999). *Student cultural diversity: Understanding and meeting the challenge* (2nd ed.). Boston: Houghton Mifflin.

Graves, M. F., & Watts-Taffe, S. M. (2002). The place of word consciousness in a research-based vocabulary program in *What research has to say about reading instruction.* Newark, DE: International Reading Association.

Hedrick, W. B., Harmon, J. M., & Linerode, P. M. (2004). Teachers' beliefs and practices of vocabulary instruction with social studies textbooks in Grades 4–8. *Reading Horizons, 45*(2), 103–125.

Hedrick, W. B., Harmon, J. M., & Linerode, P. M. (2000). Content analysis of vocabulary instruction in social studies textbooks for grades 4–8. *Elementary School Journal, 100*(3), 253–271.

Henderson, A. T., & Mapp, K. L. (2002). *A new wave of evidence: The impact of school, family, and community connections on student achievement. Annual Synthesis 2002.* National Center for Family & Community Connections with Schools. Austin: Southwest Educational Development Laboratory.

Hickman, P., Pollard-Durodola, S., & Vaughn, S. (2004). Storybook reading: Improving vocabulary and comprehension for English-language learners. *Reading Teacher, 57*(8), 720–730.

Lee, J., & Weiss, A. (2007). *The Nation's Report Card: U.S. History 2006* (NCES 2007–474). U.S. Department of Education, National Center for Education Statistics. Washington, DC: U.S. Government Printing Office.

Marzano, R. J., & Pickering, D. J. (2005). *Building Academic Vocabulary: Teacher's manual.* Alexandria, VA: ASCD.

Ogle, D., Klemp, R., & McBride, B. (2007). *Building literacy in social studies: Strategies for improving comprehension and critical thinking.* Washington, DC: Association for Supervision and Curriculum Development.

Paynter, D. E., Bodrova, E., & Doty, J. K. (2005). *For the love of words: Vocabulary instruction that works, grades K–6.* San Francisco: Jossey-Bass.

Resnick, B. (2006). Social studies market, Grades K–12. Rockaway Park, NY: Education Market Research.

Richek, M. A. (2005, February). Words are wonderful: Interactive, time-efficient strategies to teach meaning vocabulary. *Reading Teacher, 58*(5), 414–423.

Rolón, C. A. (2002/2003). Educating Latino students. *Educational Leadership, 60*(4), 40–3.

Rubinstein-Ávila, E. (2006). Connecting with Latino Learners. *Educational Leadership, 63*(5), 38–43.

Slavin, R. E., & Cheung, A. (2005). Synthesis of research on language of reading instruction for English language learners. *Review of Educational Research Summer, 75*(2), 247–284.

Tomlinson, C. A. (2004, April). Differentiation in diverse settings. *School Administrator, 61*(7).

U.S. Department of Education. (2004). *Parental involvement: Title One, Part A Non-regulatory guidance.* Washington, DC: No Child Left Behind.

U.S. Department of Education, *Building on Results: A Blueprint for Strengthening the No Child Left Behind Act,* Washington, DC, 2007.

Yarbrough, B. (2007). Why Johnny Can't Read His Textbook. *Hesperia Star.* Accessed April 25, 2007, from http://www.hesperiastar.com/onset?id=656&template=article.html.

Zelasko, N., & Antunez, B. (2000). *If your child learns in two languages: A parent's guide for improving educational opportunities for children acquiring English as a second language.* National Clearinghouse of Bilingual Education: The George Washington University: Graduate School of Education and Human Development. Washington, DC.

Zwiers, J. (2004/2005). The third language of academic English. *Educational Leadership, 62*(4), 60–63.

LESSON 1

Geography— Looking at the World

(Student Book pages 4–9)

TARGET VOCABULARY

geography the earth and the relationship between people and the earth

landform a feature of Earth's surface

climate weather in an area over a period of time

vegetation plant life

agriculture the growing of crops

fertile able to produce many crops

delta low, watery land near the mouth of a river

river system a network of streams and rivers

civilization a large, organized group of people

irrigation bringing water to dry land

COGNATES

Spanish-speaking students may find a discussion of the similarities and differences between English and Spanish cognates helpful.

English	Spanish
geography	geografía
climate	clima
vegetation	vegetación
agriculture	agricultura
fertile	fértil
delta	delta
civilization	civilización
irrigation	irrigación

Lesson Summary Geography is the study of Earth's landforms and climate, and how they affect life on Earth. Early people settled in places where crops grew best, usually flat land with a good supply of water from rivers. Often, people settled in areas with river deltas, where the soil was richest. Civilizations grew up in areas with warm climates, good water supplies, and rich soil. People used river water for irrigation.

BEFORE READING

Activate Prior Knowledge

Bring in two types of soil for students to look at and touch. The first type should be a rich, black, slightly moist soil. The other should be a grainy or pebbly sand. Ask students which soil would grow the best crops. Also ask where they think such soil would be found. Make a cluster map with the words *rich soil* in the center. Guide students to name associations with rich soil that include concepts and words such as *crops* or *agriculture, fertile, rivers, delta,* and *irrigation.*

Introduce Target Vocabulary

Tell students that they are about to read a selection about geography, a way of looking at the world. Write the target vocabulary words on the board. Model the pronunciation of each word and have student volunteers repeat the word. Discuss the meaning of each word and, if necessary, write the definition next to the word.

Present Graphic Organizer

Provide each student with a copy of Vocabulary Graphic Organizer: Word Wheel, Teacher Guide page 76. Have students choose or assign each student a target vocabulary word. As they read, students should add information about the target vocabulary word to the graphic organizer.

Word and Definition Cards
for Lesson 1 are on pages 99 and 100
of the Teacher Guide.

VOCABULARY STRATEGY: Print Features

Point out the words in bold type in the reading, and note that these are the target vocabulary words. Tell students that this book provides two ways to find the meaning of words in bold type. First, students can use context clues in the reading. These context clues usually appear near the word in bold type. Students can also use the glossary in the back of their book to find a word's meaning.

Geography—Looking at the World

geography   climate   agriculture   delta   civilization
landform   vegetation   fertile   river system   irrigation

What is the relationship between land and people? Read this selection to learn how land and people are linked.

Geography—Looking at the World

Geography and Geographers

Geography is the study of the earth and the relationship between people and the earth. Landforms are part of geography. A **landform** is a feature of Earth's surface. Mountains and valleys are landforms.

Weather is an important part of life on Earth. **Climate** is the weather in an area over a period of time. There are several different kinds of climate. Climate shapes what kind of vegetation is in an area. **Vegetation** is the plants in an area. It includes trees, bushes, and grasses. Climate also affects how many people live in an area.

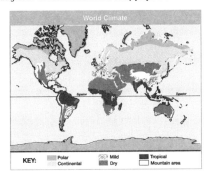

World Climate

KEY: Polar   Mild   Tropical
Continental   Dry   Mountain area

4   Geography—Looking at the World

Geographers study geography. They ask how land, people, and plants affect one another. For example, more people live in valleys than on top of mountains. Why? Valleys are warmer. They have lakes and rivers. People, plants, and animals need water to live.

Landforms That Attract Settlers

Early people settled on flat land. They could grow crops there. Growing crops is called **agriculture**. It began about 10,000 years ago. Early farmers learned that crops grew well in certain places. Land that is **fertile** is able to produce many crops.

Land in river deltas is fertile. A **delta** is low, watery land. It is formed by a fan-shaped system of streams near the mouth of a river.

Why is a delta fertile? Rich soil is carried downstream by a river system. A **river system** is a network of streams and rivers. It feeds into the main river.

Rivers begin as many fast-flowing streams. Then, they join a river. Near the river's mouth, the river flows more slowly. The river carries mud. The mud builds up. It becomes the richest farmland.

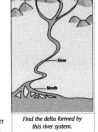

River System

River Source
River
Mouth

Find the delta formed by this river system.

Where Civilizations Form

A **civilization** is a large, organized, group of people. Many civilizations spring up along rivers. Farmers learned that they could use river water for irrigation. **Irrigation** is the process of bringing water to dry land.

Rivers also let people travel from one place to another. People began to trade goods with one another. Even today, many cities are located near sources of water. Where there is water, there is life.

Irrigation helps modern farmers grow more crops.

My Social Studies Vocabulary
Go to page 94 to list other words you have learned about geography.

Geography—Looking at the World   5

DURING READING

Read the selection aloud to students as they follow along in their book, pausing at the end of each paragraph or section. Review any words or concepts that students are having trouble understanding. Remind students that there is a glossary at the back of their book that contains all of the words that appear in boldfaced type in the lesson.

- Draw a web diagram on the board. Write *landforms* in the center circle. Have students fill in the web with the names of as many landforms as they can think of.

- Ask students what kinds of vegetation grow where they live. Ask how the climate affects the vegetation. Discuss the kinds of vegetation that do *not* grow in your area and why.

- Have students tell how irrigation is related to agriculture. Ask them how it is related to river systems. Have students make their own diagram or sketch to show this relationship. Review their drawings.

Have students read the selection again on their own.

AFTER READING

Review Graphic Organizer

Answer any questions students have about the reading selection. Then have students complete or review their graphic organizer and share it with the class.

Summarize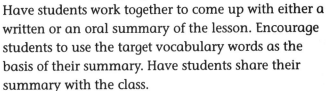

Have students work together to come up with either a written or an oral summary of the lesson. Encourage students to use the target vocabulary words as the basis of their summary. Have students share their summary with the class.

My Social Studies Vocabulary

Encourage students to turn to My Social Studies Vocabulary on page 94 of the student book and use the space provided to add other words about geography as a way of looking at the world.

ACTIVITIES A–D

Encourage students to complete as many of the activities as possible. Remind students that they may refer to the Glossary at the back of their book as they complete the activities. Students may work independently, in small groups, or as a class. When students are done, discuss the answers for each activity.

Extensions

These extension ideas allow you to reuse or expand upon the activities. Share them with students who complete the activities before other students, or have students do them for additional practice with target vocabulary words.

A   Rearrange the target vocabulary words so that they are in alphabetical order.

B   Explain why the other word choice does not make sense in the sentence.

C   Divide each target vocabulary word into syllables.

D   Choose one sentence you wrote and add two more sentences that provide more information about the topic or the target vocabulary word.

WORD ROOT

Tell students that the root geo- means "earth." Then ask them what they think geology means (geology is the study of rocks and soil.) Ask students to tell how the meaning of geology relates to the root geo.

C. *Choose the correct vocabulary word to complete each sentence.*

1. The rich soil near a river's mouth in a _____delta_____ is good for growing crops.

2. Good weather, rich soil, and water are a must for _____agriculture_____.

3. Even if crops do not get enough rain, a farmer could use _____irrigation_____ to water them.

4. When there is much rain in an area, there will be more wild _____vegetation_____.

5. Land, people, plants, and weather are all part of the study of _____geography_____.

6. A feature of Earth's surface, such as a hill or a valley, is a _____landform_____.

7. The Nile River gave rise to an advanced _____civilization_____.

8. A place's weather over time, or its _____climate_____, affects the vegetation that grows there.

9. Water flows from streams and rivers in a _____river system_____.

10. Farmers want to grow crops on land that is _____fertile_____.

Students' answers will vary.

D. *Use each word in a sentence that shows you understand the meaning of each word.*

1. agriculture — Agriculture depends on warm weather, rainfall, and good soil.

2. irrigation — Irrigation brings water to dry land.

3. vegetation — Where there is vegetation, there is a source of water.

4. civilization — A civilization will develop where people can grow enough food to feed everybody.

5. geography — Geography is the study of land features, people, plants, and climate.

6. river system — A river system connects streams to a river.

7. climate — Our climate is warm in summer and cool in winter.

8. landform — A valley is an example of a landform.

9. delta — A delta has rich soil and lots of water.

10. fertile — A farmer can grow plentiful crops in fertile soil.

Write!

Write your response to the prompt on a separate sheet of paper. Use as many vocabulary words as you can in your writing.

Geography can affect where and how people live. How do climate and landforms affect people?

Write!

Provide each student with a copy of Writing Graphic Organizer: Cause-and-Effect Chart, Teacher Guide page 80. Tell students to write their ideas about climate and landforms in the cause boxes. Then have them use the effects boxes to list the effects on people of different climates and landforms.

Sample Answer

People settle in places that can support life. More people settle in areas with fertile land, water, natural vegetation, and good climate. That way, agriculture can begin and animals can graze.

Some landforms, such as deltas, have very fertile land, and people can grow many crops. Because the land can support many people, a civilization might develop. An area with a river system can give rise to a civilization because the river system provides water for drinking, irrigation, travel, and power.

TAKE-HOME ACTIVITY

Assign the Take-Home Activity to students for additional practice with the target vocabulary words. The reproducible Take-Home Activity for Lesson 1 is on page 88 of the Teacher Guide.

Geography—Looking at the World

TAKE HOME 1

geography   climate   agriculture   delta   civilization
landform   vegetation   fertile   river system   irrigation

Use vocabulary words to complete the puzzle.

Geography—Looking at the World

ACROSS
5 plant life, including trees, bushes, and grasses
7 the study of the earth and the relationship between people and the earth
8 low, watery land formed by a fan-shaped system of streams near the mouth of a river
9 bringing water to dry land
10 the weather in an area over a period of time

DOWN
1 able to produce many crops
2 a network of streams and rivers that feed into a main river
3 a large, organized group of people
4 the growing of crops
6 a feature of Earth's surface

Tell someone in your family what you have learned about geography—looking at the world.

©Curriculum Associates, Inc. *Passwords: Social Studies Vocabulary, World Geography and Cultures, Lesson 1*

LESSON 2

The Tools of Geography

(Student Book pages 10–15)

TARGET VOCABULARY

continent one of Earth's seven major landmasses

equator an imaginary line around the middle of Earth

hemisphere half of Earth

latitude imaginary lines that circle Earth from east to west

longitude imaginary lines that run from the North Pole to the South Pole

degree a unit for measuring latitude and longitude

absolute location a place's exact location on a grid of latitude and longitude

relative location the position of one place in relation to another place

map key a guide to the lines, colors, and symbols on a map

map scale a guide to how the distances on the map compare to the actual distances on Earth

COGNATES

Spanish-speaking students may find a discussion of the similarities and differences between English and Spanish cognates helpful.

English	Spanish
continent	continente
equator	ecuador
hemisphere	hemisferio
latitude	latitud
longitude	longitud

VOCABULARY STRATEGY: Context Clues

Remind students to use context clues to find the meanings of unfamiliar words. Explain that some context clues are definition clues. Have students look on page 10 of their book to find the word *continent* and its definition. Point out that the definition for *continent* directly follows the word *is*. Explain that *is* often signals a definition clue, and have students write an equal sign above it. Then have students underline the definition that follows *is*. Have students find other examples of definition clues that begin with *is* in the text. Ask students to write an equal sign above each definition signal word and to underline each definition.

Lesson Summary Earth can be shown on a round globe or a flat map. A globe shows all of Earth's continents and bodies of water. Maps and globes have lines of latitude and longitude, which tell a place's exact, or absolute, location. A place's location in relation to another place is its relative location. A map key tells what the images, colors, and symbols stand for on a map. A map scale shows how the distances on the map compare with the actual distances on Earth.

BEFORE READING

Activate Prior Knowledge

On the board, draw a Venn diagram with the terms *map* and *globe*. Ask students how maps and globes are alike. Ask how they are different. Record their answers on the diagram. Then ask students how they would find a place on Earth. Try to solicit ideas of north or south of the equator, continent, and compass direction. Record students' ideas on the board. Review their answers as you work through the lesson.

Introduce Target Vocabulary

Tell students that they are about to read a selection about the tools of geography. Write the target vocabulary words on the board. Model the pronunciation of each word and have student volunteers repeat the word. Discuss the meaning of each word and, if necessary, write the definition next to the word.

Present Graphic Organizer

Provide each student with a copy of Vocabulary Graphic Organizer: What Is It Like? Teacher Guide page 77. Have each student choose a target vocabulary word or assign a target word to each student. As students read, they should add information about the target vocabulary word to the graphic organizer.

Word and Definition Cards
for Lesson 2 are on pages 101 and 102
of the Teacher Guide.

The Tools of Geography

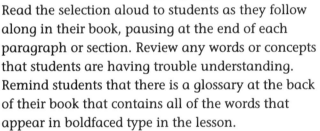

DURING READING

Read the selection aloud to students as they follow along in their book, pausing at the end of each paragraph or section. Review any words or concepts that students are having trouble understanding. Remind students that there is a glossary at the back of their book that contains all of the words that appear in boldfaced type in the lesson.

- Ask students to point out a continent on the map on page 10. Point out the six other continents. Ask students to define *continent* in their own words.

- Tell students that *hemi-* means "half." Review the term *sphere*. Note that a globe is a sphere. Ask students to use their knowledge of *hemi-* and *sphere* to define *hemisphere*.

- Review the fact that a circle has 360°. Relate degrees to other familiar units of measure, such as an inch and an ounce. Remind students that we use different units of measure for different kinds of quantities; note that distances on the surface of Earth are measured in degrees.

- Have students use a classroom map to tell the absolute and the relative location of your city or town.

Have students read the selection again on their own.

AFTER READING

Review Graphic Organizer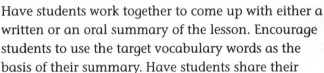

Answer any questions students have about the reading selection. Then have students complete or review their graphic organizer and share it with the class.

Summarize

Have students work together to come up with either a written or an oral summary of the lesson. Encourage students to use the target vocabulary words as the basis of their summary. Have students share their summary with the class.

My Social Studies Vocabulary

Encourage students to turn to My Social Studies Vocabulary on page 94 of the student book and use the space provided to add other words about the tools of geography.

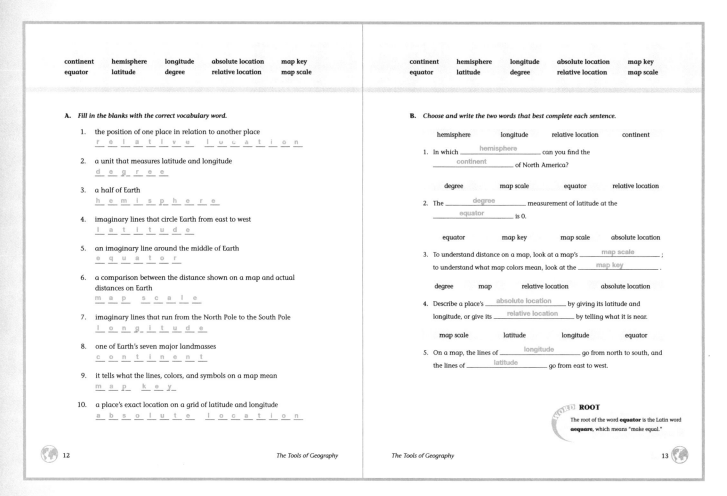

ACTIVITIES A–D

Encourage students to complete as many of the activities as possible. Remind students that they may refer to the Glossary at the back of their book as they complete the activities. Students may work independently, in small groups, or as a class. When students are done, discuss the answers for each activity.

Extensions

These extension ideas allow you to reuse or expand upon the activities. Share them with students who complete the activities before other students, or have students do them for additional practice with target vocabulary words.

A Look up two of the target vocabulary words in the Glossary, in the dictionary, and in an encyclopedia. How are the definitions similar? How are they different?

B After you have chosen the correct answers for each sentence, explain why the incorrect answers do not make sense in the sentence.

WORD ROOT

Write these words on the board and provide brief definitions for them if needed: *equal, equation, equate,* and *equidistant.* Have students relate the words' meanings to the meaning of the word *equator.*

C Make a chart with three columns. Label the columns "Imaginary Lines on a Map," "Guides on a Map," and "Places on a Map." Write the words in the correct categories. Some words can fit in more than one category.

D Choose the word on the list that is the most difficult for you to define. Make up a memory device to help you remember what the word means.

The Tools of Geography

C. *Choose the correct vocabulary word to complete each sentence.*

1. To find out how far north a place is, look at its _____latitude_____ .

2. The units of measure of latitude and longitude are the _____degree_____ , minute, and second.

3. The location of Adelaide, Australia, at 34°55'S × 138°36'E, is an _____absolute location_____ .

4. Each of Earth's seven largest land masses is a _____continent_____ .

5. If you describe Iraq as being between Iran and Saudi Arabia, you are giving Iraq's _____relative location_____ .

6. A word for "half of Earth" is _____hemisphere_____ .

7. To find the distance between two cities on a map, look at the _____map scale_____ .

8. A globe shows the _____equator_____ as being halfway between the North and South Poles.

9. To understand what colors on a map mean, look at the _____map key_____ .

10. Lines of _____longitude_____ run from the North Pole to the South Pole.

Students' answers will vary.

D. *Use each word in a sentence that shows you understand the meaning of the word.*

1. latitude ___At the equator, the latitude is 0 degrees.___

2. equator ___The imaginary line at the middle of Earth is called the equator.___

3. continent ___North America is a continent.___

4. map scale ___A map scale tells how distance on a map compares to distance on land.___

5. absolute location ___If you want the exact location of a place, find its absolute location.___

6. map key ___A map key helps people interpret maps.___

7. degree ___I wonder how many miles there are in one degree of longitude.___

8. longitude ___Lines of longitude tell how far east or west of the prime meridian a place is.___

9. relative location ___To give a general idea of where a place is, use its relative location.___

10. hemisphere ___In which hemisphere is Australia?___

Write!

Write your response to the prompt on a separate sheet of paper. Use as many vocabulary words as you can in your writing.

Suppose that a being from another world asked you how people find things on Earth. What would you say?

Write!

Provide each student with a copy of Writing Graphic Organizer: Main Idea and Details, Teacher Guide page 81. Tell students to write *maps* and *globes* in two of the main idea boxes. Then have them write details about the features or uses of each in the details boxes.

Sample Answer

People on Earth use maps and globes to show all or parts of the world's oceans and continents. Maps and globes divide our planet into north and south, using the equator as the center, and hemispheres for north and south. Then, using a grid of degrees of latitude and longitude, people can find the absolute location of a place. Or, they can give the relative location of a place by telling what it is near.

TAKE-HOME ACTIVITY

Assign the Take-Home Activity to students for additional practice with the target vocabulary words. The reproducible Take-Home Activity for Lesson 2 is on page 85 of the Teacher Guide.

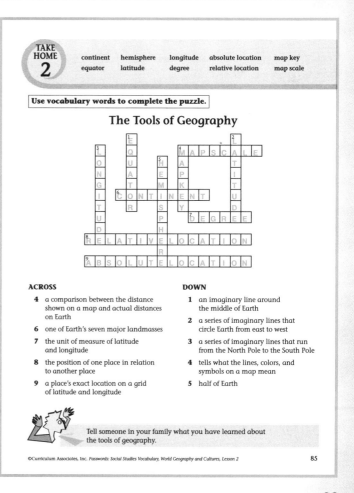

TAKE HOME 2

| continent | hemisphere | longitude | absolute location | map key |
| equator | latitude | degree | relative location | map scale |

Use vocabulary words to complete the puzzle.

The Tools of Geography

ACROSS

4 a comparison between the distance shown on a map and actual distances on Earth

6 one of Earth's seven major landmasses

7 the unit of measure of latitude and longitude

8 the position of one place in relation to another place

9 a place's exact location on a grid of latitude and longitude

DOWN

1 an imaginary line around the middle of Earth

2 a series of imaginary lines that circle Earth from east to west

3 a series of imaginary lines that run from the North Pole to the South Pole

4 tells what the lines, colors, and symbols on a map mean

5 half of Earth

Tell someone in your family what you have learned about the tools of geography.

©Curriculum Associates, Inc. Passwords: Social Studies Vocabulary, World Geography and Cultures, Lesson 2   85

LESSON 3

World Cultures

(Student Book pages 16–21)

TARGET VOCABULARY

culture the way of life of a group of people

culture region an area where many people share the same culture

government a small group of people who make the laws to rule a large group of people

economy a system in which people sell or trade goods and services

migration the movement of people from one place to another

rural a word that describes open places with few people

urban a word that describes the city

industrialization the making of goods by machine

population density the average number of people per square mile living in an area

cultural diversity a state or quality of having people from many cultures

COGNATES

Spanish-speaking students may find a discussion of the similarities and differences between English and Spanish cognates helpful.

English	Spanish
culture	cultura
government	gobierno
economy	economía
migration	migración
rural	rural
urban	urbano
industrialization	industrialización

Lesson Summary Groups of people have a common culture. A culture region is an area where many people share the same culture. Most cultures have a government and an economy. Culture changes with people's migration. Many cultures that were once rural have now become urban. Urban areas are often centers of industrialization. Urban areas have a high population density. Often, they also have cultural diversity because people from many cultures have moved there.

BEFORE READING

Activate Prior Knowledge

Ask students to make two drawings, one that shows the city and one that shows the country. When they finish, ask students to name the differences. List their responses on the board. Lead students to understand that there are more people and businesses in the city. Then ask why people might move from the country to the city, and record those responses as well. Return to their ideas as you work through the lesson.

Introduce Target Vocabulary

Tell students that they are about to read a selection about world cultures. Write the target vocabulary words on the board. Model the pronunciation of each word and have student volunteers repeat the word. Discuss the meaning of each word and, if necessary, write the definition next to the word.

Present Graphic Organizer

Provide each student with a copy of Vocabulary Graphic Organizer: Vocabulary Map, Teacher Guide page 78. Have students choose a target vocabulary word or assign one to them. As they read, students should add information to the graphic organizer above the target vocabulary word.

Word and Definition Cards
for Lesson 3 are on pages 103 and 104
of the Teacher Guide.

VOCABULARY STRATEGY: Suffixes

Point out to students that some suffixes indicate that the word is a noun. Write four common noun suffixes found in the target words: *-tion, -ion, -ment*, and *-ity*. Ask students to name the words that have these suffixes (*region, government, migration, industrialization, population density,* and *diversity*).

Explain that all of these words are nouns; they name things. Invite students to list other words they know with these suffixes and to explain why each is a noun. Encourage students to add these suffixes to the suffix chart on page 100 of their book.

culture   economy   urban   population density
culture region   migration   industrialization   cultural diversity
government   rural

What would your life be like if you lived in another place? In this passage, you'll read about how people in different places are alike and different.

World Cultures

Describing a Culture

Every community has a culture. **Culture** is the way of life of a group of people. People in a culture usually have the same religion, customs, laws, music, and art. A **culture region** is an area where many people share the same culture.

Land shapes a people's culture. In East Africa, the climate is hot and dry. The land is flat grassland with few trees. Homes of the Maasai are built of mud, not wood. Families own cattle. The cattle graze on the grassland.

Cattle are central to the life of the Maasai.

Government and Economy

Cultures are influenced by a government. A **government** is a small group of people who make laws to rule a large group of people.

Cultures are also influenced by the economy of a country or region. An **economy** is a system in which people sell or trade goods and services. A strong economy depends on having goods to buy and people with money.

Governments and economies are different from place to place. Both affect what people's lives will be like.

Cultures Change

Cultures change when people move. **Migration** is the movement of people from one place to another. They can move from one country to another. They can move within a country.

At one time, most of the world's people lived in rural areas. A **rural** area has many open spaces and few people. Many people in rural areas are farmers.

Now, more people live in **urban**, or city, areas. People move to urban areas for work. **Industrialization** is the making of many goods by machine. It creates many jobs. So, the population density is greater in urban areas. **Population density** is the average number of people per square mile living in an area.

This urban area has a high population density.

This desert region has a low population density.

People from many different cultures often move into the same area. Such an area with people from many cultures has **cultural diversity**.

 My World Geography Vocabulary
Go to page 94 to list other words you have learned about world cultures.

DURING READING

Read the selection aloud to students as they follow along in their book, pausing at the end of each paragraph or section. Review any words or concepts that students are having trouble understanding. Remind students that there is a glossary at the back of their book that contains all of the words that appear in boldfaced type in the lesson.

- Talk about how groups of people share a way of life. Write the word *culture* on the board, and explain that your classroom is an example of a small culture. Ask: What is our way of life? What do we share or use in common? Students may mention language; goals; activities; school policies and rules; tools, such as computers and pens; or shared customs, such as saying the Pledge of Allegiance together.

- Ask students to name a culture region and to give a reason for their answer.

- Write and say the phrases "laws and rules," "buying and selling," "people moving to a new place," and "making many goods by machine." Have students match the phrases to the terms *government, economy, migration,* and *industrialization.*

- Ask students to name places they know or have visited that are urban or rural. Elicit reasons for their choices.

Have students read the selection again on their own.

AFTER READING

Review Graphic Organizer

Answer any questions students have about the reading selection. Then have students complete or review their graphic organizer and share it with the class.

Summarize

Have students work together to come up with either a written or an oral summary of the lesson. Encourage students to use the target vocabulary words as the basis of their summary. Have students share their summary with the class.

My Social Studies Vocabulary

Encourage students to turn to My Social Studies Vocabulary on page 94 of the student book and use the space provided to add other words about world cultures.

culture   economy   urban   population density
culture region   migration   industrialization   cultural diversity
government   rural

A. *Fill in the blanks with the correct vocabulary word.*

1. a system in which people sell or trade goods and services
   e c o n o m y

2. the movement of people from one place to another
   m i g r a t i o n

3. related to the city
   u r b a n

4. an area where many people share the same culture
   c u l t u r e   r e g i o n

5. the making of many goods by machine
   i n d u s t r i a l i z a t i o n

6. the state that results from having many cultures in the same area
   c u l t u r a l   d i v e r s i t y

7. the way of life of a group of people
   c u l t u r e

8. the average number of people per square mile living in an area
   p o p u l a t i o n   d e n s i t y

9. related to open space or countryside
   r u r a l

10. a small group of people who make laws and rule a large group of people
    g o v e r n m e n t

---

culture   economy   urban   population density
culture region   migration   industrialization   cultural diversity
government   rural

B. *Circle the word that makes sense in each sentence. Then write the word.*

1. What businesses offer and what people buy creates an (industrialization, (economy))   economy

2. People follow laws made by their (culture region, (government)).   government

3. Getting a better job is one reason for people's (urban, (migration)) to cities.   migration

4. There are many people living closely together in ((urban,) rural) areas.   urban

5. When people in an area share the same language, religion, laws, and customs, they are in a ((culture region,) migration).   culture region

6. When an area has ((cultural diversity,) population density), people from many cultures live there.   cultural diversity

7. Cities have a greater ((population density,) government) than rural areas have.   population density

8. Cities often grow as a result of (culture, (industrialization)).   industrialization

9. People who have the same way of life have the same (cultural diversity, (culture)).   culture

10. Almost all farmers live in ((rural,) economy) areas.   rural

ROOT
The word **culture** comes from the Latin word **cultus**, which means "care for" or "tend."

ACTIVITIES A–D

Encourage students to complete as many of the activities as possible. Remind students that they may refer to the Glossary at the back of their book as they complete the activities. Students may work independently, in small groups, or as a class. When students are done, discuss the answers for each activity.

Extensions

These extension ideas allow you to reuse or expand upon the activities. Share them with students who complete the activities before other students, or have students do them for additional practice with target vocabulary words.

A Put the target vocabulary words in alphabetical order.

B Rewrite each sentence as a question.

WORD ROOT

Tell students that other words that share the same root with *culture* are *cultivate* and *agriculture*. Have students look up the words in a dictionary and explain their connection to the Latin root.

C Choose one of the target vocabulary words and use it to create a poem about the word. Write the word vertically down a sheet of paper, one letter per line. Have that letter serve as the first letter of the first word of that line of the poem.

D Circle the verbs and underline the nouns in each sentence.

culture	economy	urban	population density
culture region	migration	industrialization	cultural diversity
government	rural		

C. *Choose the correct vocabulary word to complete each pair of sentences.*

1. A city with people from 50 countries has ___cultural diversity___.
   Many languages are spoken in an area with ___cultural diversity___.
2. That area is a ___culture region___ because its people all have the same culture.
   North Africa is a ___culture region___ because its people have the same background.
3. A group's language, religion, and customs are part of its ___culture___.
   A group of people's way of life is their ___culture___.
4. A farm would be in a ___rural___ area.
   You would not find any cities in a ___rural___ area.
5. The number of people in an area is its ___population density___.
   A city has a high ___population density___.
6. Factories and jobs were created by the rise of ___industrialization___.
   People moved to city areas because of ___industrialization___.
7. The opposite of *rural* is ___urban___.
   Cities are ___urban___ areas.
8. When people have good jobs and money to spend, the ___economy___ is strong.
   The buying and selling of goods and services make up a place's ___economy___.
9. Jobs in cities created a ___migration___ to cities from farms.
   To get away from war is a reason for ___migration___.
10. A group's laws are made by its ___government___.
    A culture is influenced by its ___government___.

 20   World Cultures

---

culture	economy	urban	population density
culture region	migration	industrialization	cultural diversity
government	rural		

Students' answers will vary.
D. *Use each pair of words in a sentence.*

1. culture region, cultural diversity
   The people in a culture region have little cultural diversity.
   _____
   _____

2. culture, government
   People in every culture have a form of government.
   _____
   _____

3. urban, population density
   Urban areas have a high population density.
   _____
   _____

4. industrialization, migration
   Industrialization led to a migration to cities to find jobs.
   _____
   _____

5. rural, economy
   The economy in a rural area would be different from that in the city
   because there would be fewer businesses.
   _____

 Write!
Write your response to the prompt on a separate sheet of paper.
Use as many vocabulary words as you can in your writing.

How might two people from different cultures be alike and different?

World Cultures   21

Write! 🖊

Provide each student with a copy of Writing Graphic Organizer: Two-Column Chart, Teacher Guide page 82. Tell students to label the headings "Similarities" and "Differences" and to list their ideas in the correct column.

Sample Answer

   Two people from different cultures might be different in the way they look, dress, and speak. They may have different religions, beliefs, and backgrounds. Their music and art might be different, too. One person might live in an urban area with industrialization, a high population density, and cultural diversity. The other might live in a rural area with no cultural diversity.

   They both have a government, but the form of government would probably be different. Both cultures would have some sort of economy, but the economies would probably be different, too. The thing that they definitely have in common is that they are both human.

TAKE-HOME ACTIVITY 📖🖊🗣

Assign the Take-Home Activity to students for additional practice with the target vocabulary words. The reproducible Take-Home Activity for Lesson 3 is on page 86 of the Teacher Guide.

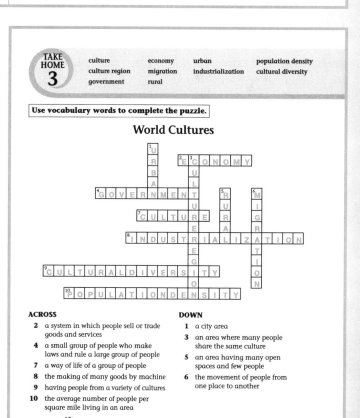

LESSON 4

The United States and Canada

(Student Book pages 22–27)

TARGET VOCABULARY

natural resource something in nature that people can use

mountain range a long chain of mountains

tributary a stream that joins others and flows into a river or lake

plain a flat land with few trees

standard of living a measure of the quality of life

immigrant someone who comes to a country to live

capitalism an economic system in which private owners control and use resources

market economy an economy in which business owners compete with one another to sell goods and services

technology a way of using new ideas and machines to create things that make people's lives better

free trade the selling of goods from one country to another without taxes

COGNATES

Spanish-speaking students may find a discussion of the similarities and differences between English and Spanish cognates helpful.

English	Spanish
natural resource	recursos naturales
tributary	tributario
immigrant	inmigrante
capitalism	capitalismo
technology	tecnología

Lesson Summary Much of the wealth of the United States and Canada comes from natural resources. Both countries have many waterways, forests, and large plains where crops grow well. Both countries are also nations of immigrants. They have high standards of living, which are the result, in part, of strong, lasting governments. The economic system in both countries is capitalism. It creates a market economy that encourages the production of goods and the development of new technology.

BEFORE READING

Activate Prior Knowledge

Explain that this lesson is about the United States and Canada. Then have students write each target vocabulary word one by one, and have students rate their knowledge of it on a scale: Know it, Think I have some idea of what it means, or Do not know it all. Return to this list after reading to discuss how their knowledge of each word has changed.

Introduce Target Vocabulary

Tell students that they are about to read a selection about the United States and Canada. Write the target vocabulary words on the board. Model the pronunciation of each word and have student volunteers repeat the word. Discuss the meaning of each word and, if necessary, write the definition next to the word.

Present Graphic Organizer

Provide each student with a copy of Vocabulary Graphic Organizer: Word Web, Teacher Guide page 79. Have students choose or assign each student a target vocabulary word. Tell students to write this word in the center circle. As they read, students should add information about the target vocabulary word in the outer circles.

Word and Definition Cards
for Lesson 4 are on pages 105 and 106
of the Teacher Guide.

VOCABULARY STRATEGY: Multiple-Meaning Words

Explain to students that knowing more than one meaning of a word can help them expand their vocabulary. Ask students if they know other meanings for the target vocabulary word *plain* (*not special, simple, clear, not pretty*). Discuss the different meanings of *plain* and have students write a sentence illustrating each meaning.

The United States and Canada

natural resource   plain   capitalism   technology
mountain range   standard of living   market economy   free trade
tributary   immigrant

How much do you know about the country you live in? What do you know about neighboring countries? Read this selection to learn about the land and people of the United States and Canada.

The United States and Canada

A Richness of Natural Resources

The United States and Canada are rich nations. Much of their wealth comes from having many natural resources. A **natural resource** is something in nature that people can use. It can be water, soil, trees, minerals, or oil.

Both countries get some of their water from rain and melted snow that drains from mountain ranges. A **mountain range** is a long chain of mountains. When water reaches the land below the mountains, it forms tributaries. A **tributary** is a stream that joins others and flows into a river or lake. These waterways provide water to drink and to water crops.

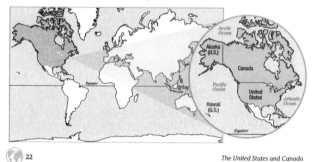

Both countries also have vast plains. A **plain**, also called a prairie, is a flat land with few trees. The Great Plains in the United States and the Interior Plains in Canada have fertile soil.

The western area of both countries is rich in forests. They supply wood for building. Both countries also have minerals, such as copper and iron, and oil.

The United States and Canada Today

Both the United States and Canada have a high standard of living. A **standard of living** is a measure of the quality of life. A high standard of living includes having good food, housing, education, and healthcare. The high standard of living attracts many immigrants. An **immigrant** is someone who comes to a country to live.

The high standard of living is due to three reasons. First, both countries have many natural resources. Second, both have stable governments. Third, both governments favor capitalism. In **capitalism**, private owners control and use resources for profit.

Capitalism creates a **market economy**. Business owners compete with one another to sell goods and services. Capitalism also encourages a growth in technology. **Technology** is the use of new ideas and machines to improve people's lives. Common technologies are automotive, medical, and computers.

The United States and Canada work together to make their economies stronger. They now have a free trade agreement. **Free trade** is the selling of goods from one country to another without taxes. This has made goods cheaper to buy.

Mineral Deposits in the United States and Canada

KEY:
Oil   Coal
Uranium   Lead & Zinc   Copper
Silver   Iron   Gold

Leaders from the United States, Canada, and Mexico sign a free trade agreement.

My World Geography Vocabulary
Go to page 95 to list other words you have learned about the United States and Canada.

22   *The United States and Canada*

The United States and Canada   23

DURING READING

Read the selection aloud to students as they follow along in their book, pausing at the end of each paragraph or section. Review any words or concepts that students are having trouble understanding. Remind students that there is a glossary at the back of their book that contains all of the words that appear in boldfaced type in the lesson.

- Ask students where they would find natural resources. Have them give examples of natural resources.

- Point out to students that some of the vocabulary words are open compounds: two or more words describe one idea. Have students identify the target vocabulary words that are open compounds and then help them to define each word of the compound words.

- Ask students to name some things that people with a high standard of living enjoy.

- Write the word *capitalism* at the center of a cluster. Have students name words that help tell what capitalism is. Elicit the terms *competition, market*

economy, and *producing goods*. Relate the idea of capitalism to using technology.

Have students read the selection again on their own.

AFTER READING

Review Graphic Organizer

Answer any questions students have about the reading selection. Then have students complete or review their graphic organizer and share it with the class.

Summarize

Have students work together to come up with either a written or an oral summary of the lesson. Encourage students to use the target vocabulary words as the basis of their summary. Have students share their summary with the class.

My Social Studies Vocabulary

Encourage students to turn to My Social Studies Vocabulary on page 95 of the student book and use the space provided to add other words about the United States and Canada.

The United States and Canada

natural resource   plain   capitalism   technology
mountain range   standard of living market economy   free trade
tributary   immigrant

A. Match each word with its meaning. Write the letter of the correct meaning on the line in front of each word.

1. __j__ standard of living
2. __e__ market economy
3. __h__ free trade
4. __g__ mountain range
5. __i__ natural resource
6. __f__ capitalism
7. __b__ technology
8. __c__ tributary
9. __d__ immigrant
10. __a__ plain

a. a flat land with few trees

b. the use of new ideas and machines to improve people's lives

c. a stream that joins others and flows into a river or lake

d. someone who comes to a country to live

e. a system in which business owners compete with one another to sell goods and services

f. an economic system in which private owners control and use resources for profit

g. a long chain of mountains

h. the selling of goods from one country to another without taxes

i. something in nature that people can use

j. a measure of the quality of life

natural resource   plain   capitalism   technology
mountain range   standard of living market economy   free trade
tributary   immigrant

B. Circle the word that makes sense in each sentence. Then write the word.

1. People might grow crops on a (mountain range, **plain**) because the soil is fertile. _____plain_____

2. A person who moves from Canada to France to live is an (standard of living, **immigrant**). _____immigrant_____

3. When rain drains from a mountain range, it might form a stream that becomes a (**tributary**, natural resource) to a river. _____tributary_____

4. When people have everything they need to have a good life, they have a high (capitalism, **standard of living**) _____standard of living_____

5. When businesses compete to sell goods and services, that creates a (**market economy**, immigrant). _____market economy_____

6. A mineral is a (**natural resource** technology). _____natural resource_____

7. Americans who buy Canada's goods will pay less than they once did because of a (**free trade**, market economy) agreement. _____free trade_____

8. The Rocky Mountains are a (**mountain range** tributary) in the United States and Canada. _____mountain range_____

9. Business owners in the United States and Canada can decide what to make and sell because their countries believe in (free trade, **capitalism**) _____capitalism_____

10. American and Canadian citizens have many new kinds of products because of (plain, **technology**). _____technology_____

ROOT
The word **plain** comes from the Latin word **planus**, which means "flat."

ACTIVITIES A–D

Encourage students to complete as many of the activities as possible. Remind students that they may refer to the Glossary at the back of their book as they complete the activities. Students may work independently, in small groups, or as a class. When students are done, discuss the answers for each activity.

Extensions

These extension ideas allow you to reuse or expand upon the activities. Share them with students who complete the activities before other students, or have students do them for additional practice with target vocabulary words.

A Write each word meaning as a complete sentence.

B On a sheet of graph paper, create a word search puzzle using the target vocabulary words. Exchange papers with a partner and solve your partner's puzzle.

WORD ROOT

Discuss with students how the meaning of *airplane*, *plane* (as in the tool that makes things flat), and *inclined plane* are related to the root word *planus*.

C Many of the target vocabulary words contain smaller words. For example, words that you can make from *market economy* include *make, mom, acorn, arm, army, yet, key*, and *rock*. Make a list of all the smaller words you can find in one target vocabulary word.

D Draw a picture or diagram to illustrate one of the target vocabulary words.

natural resource   plain   capitalism   technology
mountain range   standard of living   market economy   free trade
tributary   immigrant

C. *Choose the correct vocabulary word to complete each sentence.*

1. If a government encourages _____capitalism_____ , some people will start a business.

2. Businesses compete with one another in a _____market economy_____ .

3. People in the United States and Canada can buy each other's products without taxes because of a _____free trade_____ agreement.

4. People have a wide variety of new products because of _____technology_____ .

5. Oil is an important _____natural resource_____ in the United States and Canada.

6. In the United States or Canada, an _____immigrant_____ might meet many other people from the country from which she moved.

7. People who are poor, have little food, and live in shacks have a low _____standard of living_____ .

8. One source of water is melted snow from a _____mountain range_____ .

9. Another name for a prairie is a _____plain_____ .

10. Water flows into a river or lake from a _____tributary_____ .

26   *The United States and Canada*

---

natural resource   plain   capitalism   technology
mountain range   standard of living   market economy   free trade
tributary   immigrant

Students' answers will vary.
D. *Use each word in a sentence that shows you understand the meaning of the word.*

1. tributary ___A tributary brings water from high ground to a river or lake.___

2. immigrant ___Mr. Nguyen is an immigrant from Vietnam.___

3. capitalism ___Capitalism can make people rich because they can own a business and make a profit.___

4. plain ___A person could grow crops on a plain because it is flat and has good soil.___

5. mountain range ___A mountain range can provide water to the land below it.___

6. market economy ___Businesses compete with one another for sales in a market economy.___

7. standard of living ___The United States has a high standard of living because so many of its people live well.___

8. free trade ___A free trade agreement lets Americans buy Canada's goods tax free.___

9. natural resource ___Coal is a natural resource.___

10. technology ___Computers are the best use of technology.___

Write!
Write your response to the prompt on a separate sheet of paper. Use as many vocabulary words as you can in your writing.
What are some things the United States and Canada have in common?

The United States and Canada   27

Write!

Provide each student with a copy of Writing Graphic Organizer: Two-Column Chart, Teacher Guide page 82. Tell students to write "The United States" at the top of one column and "Canada" at the top of the other column. They should then jot down information and facts about each country in the appropriate column.

Sample Answer

The United States and Canada have many things in common. Their people are, for the most part, immigrants. They enjoy a high standard of living and the benefits of technology.

Both countries have rich natural resources. Both governments encourage capitalism and a market economy. They have a free-trade agreement to boost their economies.

There are also similar landforms, such as mountain ranges and plains.

TAKE-HOME ACTIVITY

Assign the Take-Home Activity to students for additional practice with the target vocabulary words. The reproducible Take-Home Activity for Lesson 4 is on page 87 of the Teacher Guide.

The United States and Canada

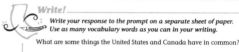

TAKE HOME 4

natural resource   plain   capitalism   technology
mountain range   standard of living   market economy   free trade
tributary   immigrant

Use vocabulary words to complete the puzzle.

The United States and Canada

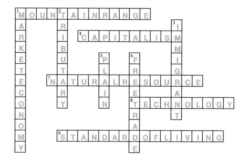

ACROSS

1 a long chain of mountains

4 an economic system in which private owners control and use resources for profit

7 something in nature that people can use

8 the use of new ideas and machines to improve people's lives

9 a measure of the quality of life

DOWN

1 when business owners compete with one another to sell goods and services

2 a stream that joins others and flows into a river or lake

3 someone who comes to a country to live

5 a flat land with few trees

6 the selling of goods from one country to another without taxes

 Tell someone in your family what you have learned about the United States and Canada.

©Curriculum Associates, Inc. *Passwords: Social Studies Vocabulary, World Geography and Cultures, Lesson 4*   87

The United States and Canada   **31**

LESSON 5

Latin America

(Student Book pages 28–33)

TARGET VOCABULARY

volcano an opening in Earth's crust through which liquid rock and gases flow

elevation height

plateau a high, flat landform

tropical climate weather that is always very warm and moist

colonization the making of settlements in another land

descendant someone related to a person who lived long ago

developing country a country that is moving from an economy based on farming to one based on industry

cash crop a crop that is raised to sell

export a good that is sold to another country

deforestation the cutting down of a forest

COGNATES

Spanish-speaking students may find a discussion of the similarities and differences between English and Spanish cognates helpful.

English	Spanish
volcano	volcán
elevation	elevación
tropical climate	clima tropical
colonization	colonización
descendant	descendiente
export	exportación

Lesson Summary Latin America has a wide variety of landforms, including volcanoes, high mountains, plateaus, and tropical rain forests. Spain and Portugal colonized much of Latin America. As a result of colonization, most people in Latin America speak Spanish or Portuguese and are Catholic. Many Latin American nations are developing countries. Deforestation results when farmers clear land to grow cash crops for export.

BEFORE READING

Activate Prior Knowledge

Make a grid with eight boxes. Label them A–C, D–F, G–I, J–L, M–O, P–R, S–V, and W–Z. Then ask students to tell what they know about the climate, landforms, and economy of Latin America. Record their answers in the grid; for example, record *Spanish language* in the box labeled S–V. After reading, ask students to add other topics and target words to the grid.

Introduce Target Vocabulary

Tell students that they are about to read a selection about Latin America. Write the target vocabulary words on the board. Model the pronunciation of each word and have student volunteers repeat the word. Discuss the meaning of each word and, if necessary, write the definition next to the word.

Present Graphic Organizer

Provide each student with a copy of Vocabulary Graphic Organizer: Word Wheel, Teacher Guide page 76. Have students choose a target vocabulary word or assign one to them. Tell students to write this word in the center circle. As students read, they should add information about the target vocabulary word on the spokes of the wheel.

Word and Definition Cards
for Lesson 5 are on pages 107 and 108
of the Teacher Guide.

VOCABULARY STRATEGY: Context Clues

Ask students what words may signal a context clue (*is, is called, means*). Note that *or* may also be a signal word. Have students find the word *elevation* on page 28 and the word *or* that follows it. Have them circle *or* and underline the definition of *elevation*. Call attention to the commas that enclose the definition. Note that sometimes only commas signal a word's definition. Have students find *plateau* on page 28 and circle the comma that immediately follows *plateau*. Then have them find the next comma and circle it. Note that the commas enclose the meaning of *plateau*. Ask students to find another word in the reading that uses the same kind of comma context clue (*deforestation*).

Latin America

volcano   tropical climate   developing country   export
elevation   colonization   cash crop   deforestation
plateau   descendant

*Latin America includes Mexico, Central America, the Caribbean, and
South America. It is called "Latin" America because the languages that
are spoken there, Spanish and Portuguese, have their roots in Latin.*

Latin America

Lands of Great Variety

Latin America has amazing landforms! For instance, Mexico
and Central America have volcanoes. A **volcano** is an opening in
Earth's crust through which liquid rock and gases flow.

The Andes Mountains are amazing too. They are among the
highest mountains in the world. The **elevation**, or height, of some
mountains reaches almost 23,000 feet.

A vast **plateau**, a high, flat landform, covers much of central
Mexico. The soil is very rich. But the area gets little rain.

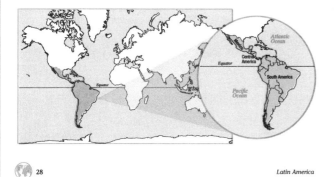

Much of Latin America has a tropical
climate. A **tropical climate** is always very
warm and moist. Parts of Central and South
America have tropical rain forests. These are
lush, dense forests. They get as much as 260
inches of rain per year! The rain creates vast
rivers. One is the Amazon in Brazil.

A Spanish-Portuguese Past

Once, only Native Americans lived in Latin
America. In the 1500s, people from Spain and
Portugal began to build settlements. This was
the beginning of **colonization**. The Spanish
and Portuguese brought African slaves to Latin
America. Now, many Latin Americans are
descendants of Native Americans, early settlers,
and former slaves. A **descendant** is someone
related to an earlier person or group.

The effect of these early settlers remains
today. Most people speak Spanish. In Brazil,
Portuguese is a common language. Also, most
people are Catholic, a Christian religion. It
was the religion of the early settlers.

Catholic churches can be found in almost every city
and town in Latin America.

Latin America Today

Many countries have a low standard
of living. Their people have no electricity
or running water. Harsh military leaders
run some countries. Poorer countries are
called developing countries. A **developing
country** is moving from an economy based
on farming to one based on industry.

Most countries try to increase their wealth
by selling cash crops for export. A **cash crop**
is a crop that is raised to sell. An **export** is
a good that is sold to another country. Cash
crops include coffee, bananas, pineapples, and
sugar cane.

Farmers cut down
tropical forests to
grow cash crops.
But **deforestation**,
the cutting down
of forests, also kills
many plants and
animals.

Some countries,
such as Costa
Rica, are stopping
deforestation. Why?
Because people will
travel there to see the plants and animals in
tropical forests. They bring in more money
than growing cash crops in deforested areas!

*Deforestation has
reduced the size of the
tropical forest.*

My World Geography Vocabulary
Go to page 95 to list other words you have learned
about Latin America.

DURING READING

Read the selection aloud to students as they follow
along in their book, pausing at the end of each
paragraph or section. Review any words or concepts
that students are having trouble understanding.
Remind students that there is a glossary at the back
of their book that contains all of the words that
appear in boldfaced type in the lesson.

- Have students draw or sketch the following: an
  active volcano, mountains with a high elevation and
  mountains with a low elevation, and a plateau.

- Draw a Venn diagram to compare and contrast the
  terms *cash crop* and *export*. Have students name
  similarities and differences.

- Have students name other words in the word
  family for *colonization* (*colony, colonize, colonist,
  colonial*). Do the same for *deforestation* (*forest,
  forested, deforest*). Talk about how the words in
  each family are related.

Have students read the selection again on their own.

AFTER READING

Review Graphic Organizer

Answer any questions students have about the reading
selection. Then have students complete or review their
graphic organizer and share it with the class.

Summarize

Have students work together to come up with either a
written or an oral summary of the lesson. Encourage
students to use the target vocabulary words as the
basis of their summary. Have students share their
summary with the class.

My Social Studies Vocabulary

Encourage students to turn to My Social Studies
Vocabulary on page 95 of the student book and use the
space provided to add other words about Latin America.

volcano	tropical climate	developing country	export
elevation	colonization	cash crop	deforestation
plateau	descendant		

A. *Match each word with its meaning. Write the letter of the correct meaning on the line in front of each word.*

1. __c__ developing country
2. __g__ tropical climate
3. __i__ deforestation
4. __h__ colonization
5. __b__ descendant
6. __a__ cash crop
7. __j__ volcano
8. __f__ plateau
9. __e__ export
10. __d__ elevation

a. a crop that is raised to sell

b. someone related to an earlier person or group

c. a country that is moving from an economy based on farming to one based on industry

d. height, as in the measure of mountains

e. a good that is sold to another country

f. a high, flat landform

g. weather that is always very warm and moist

h. the setting up of settlements in another country

i. the cutting down of forests

j. an opening in Earth's crust through which rock and gases flow

---

volcano	tropical climate	developing country	export
elevation	colonization	cash crop	deforestation
plateau	descendant		

B. *Choose and write the two words that best complete each sentence.*

| plateau | tropical climate | volcano | export |

1. In Mexico, you might see a _____volcano_____ spewing liquid rock or a high, flat _____plateau_____ .

| deforestation | elevation | tropical climate | plateau |

2. Rain forests are found in areas with a ____tropical climate____ where the _____elevation_____ is usually low.

| volcano | export | colonization | cash crop |

3. Coffee can be grown as a ____cash crop____ and then sold as an ____export____ to other countries.

| deforestation | elevation | descendant | developing country |

4. Stopping ____deforestation____ might make a ____developing country____ richer.

| descendant | developing country | colonization | cash crop |

5. A Native American is not the ____descendant____ of a Spanish settler involved in the ____colonization____ of the region.

WORD ROOT

The root of **export** is the Latin word **portare**, which means "carry."

ACTIVITIES A–D

Encourage students to complete as many of the activities as possible. Remind students that they may refer to the Glossary at the back of their book as they complete the activities. Students may work independently, in small groups, or as a class. When students are done, discuss the answers for each activity.

Extensions

These extension ideas allow you to reuse or expand upon the activities. Share them with students who complete the activities before other students, or have students do them for additional practice with target vocabulary words.

A Write the number of syllables in each vocabulary word.

B Choose two target vocabulary words that were not paired and write a new sentence using them.

WORD ROOT

Write and say *import*. Explain that the prefix *im-* can mean "in." Have students compare and contrast the prefixes, root words, and meanings of *export* and *import*. Discuss how the following words have meanings related to the Latin root *portare: porter, transportation,* and *portable.*

C Write five target words that have a word part (prefix, suffix, root word, or base word) that is familiar to you. Underline the word part. Next to the target word, write another word you know with the same word part.

D Rewrite your sentences, but leave blanks for the vocabulary words. Exchange papers with a partner, and see if you both can fill in the correct words missing from each other's sentences.

volcano   tropical climate   developing country   export
elevation   colonization   cash crop   deforestation
plateau   descendant

C. *Choose the correct vocabulary word to complete each pair of sentences.*

1. Land that is high and flat is a _____plateau_____.
   Central Mexico has a large, flat _____plateau_____.
2. Sugar grown for sale is a _____cash crop_____.
   A farmer sells a _____cash crop_____ instead of eating it.
3. The climate in Central America is a _____tropical climate_____.
   People who like heat and rain like Central America's _____tropical climate_____.
4. The Spanish and Portuguese led the _____colonization_____ of Latin America.
   Making a settlement is the first step in _____colonization_____.
5. An opening in Earth's crust through which liquid rock can pour is a _____volcano_____.
   In Mexico, you might see a _____volcano_____ spilling out liquid rock.
6. A person who is a _____descendant_____ of Spanish people may speak Spanish, too.
   A Latin American is probably a _____descendant_____ of one of three early groups.
7. A country that is moving from agriculture to industry is a _____developing country_____.
   Peru is a _____developing country_____ in Latin America.
8. The United States might buy an _____export_____ from Latin America.
   Countries can get richer by selling a crop as an _____export_____.
9. A mountain with a high _____elevation_____ may have snow on top.
   A plain has a low _____elevation_____.
10. Plants and animals die when _____deforestation_____ happens.
    Where there is _____deforestation_____, the land is bare.

 32   *Latin America*

---

volcano   tropical climate   developing country   export
elevation   colonization   cash crop   deforestation
plateau   descendant

Students' answers will vary.

D. *Use each word in a sentence that shows you understand the meaning of the word.*

1. cash crop _If farmers don't need to eat the food they grow, they can sell it as a cash crop._
2. colonization _The colonization of Latin America by the Spanish has had a lasting effect._
3. deforestation _Deforestation destroys forests and everything in them._
4. developing country _Bolivia is a developing country that is trying to improve the life of its people._
5. elevation _Latin America has tall mountains with high elevation._
6. export _Latin American countries grow fruit that they export._
7. descendant _I am a descendant of Chinese immigrants._
8. plateau _A plateau is high, like a mountain, but flat on top._
9. tropical climate _A tropical climate would feel hot and sticky._
10. volcano _An active volcano spilling out liquid rock could be dangerous._

Write!
Write your response to the prompt on a separate sheet of paper. Use as many vocabulary words as you can in your writing.

Would you like to visit Latin America? Why or why not?

Latin America   33

Write!

Provide each student with a copy of Writing Graphic Organizer: Main Idea and Details, Teacher Guide page 81. Tell students to use the Main Idea boxes to write reasons why they would or would not like to visit Latin America. Ask them to use the Details boxes to provide support for their reasons.

Sample answer

Latin America would be great to visit. I'd like to see a volcano spewing liquid rock, the mountains with the highest elevation, and the Amazon River. I'd like to see the plants and animals in a tropical forest before deforestation kills everything in it. I'd like to eat ripe pineapples fresh from the tree, before they are sold as a cash crop for export.

However, because so many people are descendants of Spanish and Portuguese settlers, I might have a hard time with their languages. Also, the tropical climate might be hot and sticky.

TAKE-HOME ACTIVITY

Assign the Take-Home Activity to students for additional practice with the target vocabulary words. The reproducible Take-Home Activity for Lesson 5 is on page 88 of the Teacher Guide.

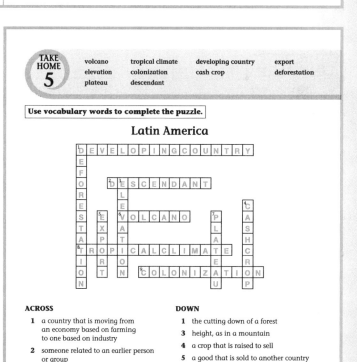

TAKE HOME 5

volcano   tropical climate   developing country   export
elevation   colonization   cash crop   deforestation
plateau   descendant

Use vocabulary words to complete the puzzle.

Latin America

ACROSS
1. a country that is moving from an economy based on farming to one based on industry
2. someone related to an earlier person or group
6. an opening in Earth's crust through which rock and gases flow
8. weather that is always very warm and moist
9. the making of settlements in another land

DOWN
1. the cutting down of a forest
3. height, as in a mountain
4. a crop that is raised to sell
5. a good that is sold to another country
7. a high, flat landform

Tell someone in your family what you have learned about Latin America.

88   ©Curriculum Associates, Inc. *Passwords: Social Studies Vocabulary, World Geography and Cultures, Lesson 5*

Latin America   35

LESSON 6

Europe

(Student Book pages 34–39)

TARGET VOCABULARY

peninsula an area of land that is mostly surrounded by water

channel a narrow sea between two large areas of land

ethnic group a group of people who have common ancestors, history, language, and way of life

ethnic conflict fighting among ethnic groups

border an imaginary line that separates countries

manufacturing the making of goods by machine

service industry a group of businesses that provide services

tourism the business of helping people travel on vacations

European Union a group of countries in Europe that are working together

common currency a system of money that is shared by different countries

COGNATES

Spanish-speaking students may find a discussion of the similarities and differences between English and Spanish cognates helpful.

English	Spanish
peninsula	península
channel	canal
ethnic group	grupo étnico
border	borde
manufacturing	manufactura
service industry	industria de servicios
tourism	turismo

Lesson Summary Three large peninsulas form Europe. A channel separates the island nation of Great Britain from the mainland. Many ethnic groups live in Europe, and there have been many ethnic conflicts there. Over the years, many national borders have changed. Many nations depend on manufacturing as well as on service industries, such as tourism. Many countries have joined the European Union. These countries have a common currency.

BEFORE READING

Activate Prior Knowledge

Ask students whether the following statements are true or false:

- Water surrounds most of Europe.
- Europe has many different climates.
- Europe has many different groups with common histories, language, and other ways of life.

Use a map to point out Europe's geography and help students to see how the statements are true.

Introduce Target Vocabulary

Tell students that they are about to read a selection about Europe. Write the target vocabulary words on the board. Model the pronunciation of each word and have student volunteers repeat the word. Discuss the meaning of each word and, if necessary, write the definition next to the word.

Present Graphic Organizer

Provide each student with a copy of Vocabulary Graphic Organizer: What Is It Like? Teacher Guide page 77. Have each student choose a target vocabulary word or assign a word to each student. Tell students to write their word in the center box. As students read, they should complete the graphic organizer.

Word and Definition Cards
for Lesson 6 are on pages 109 and 110
of the Teacher Guide.

VOCABULARY STRATEGY: Multiple-Meaning Words

Write the target vocabulary word *channel* on the board. Ask students what meaning or meanings they know for the word *channel* (*television channel*). Explain that *channel* is a multiple-meaning word. Discuss the meaning students will learn in this lesson: a narrow sea between two large areas of land.

Ask students if they can identify another multiple-meaning word in the word list (*border*). Ask for meanings of *border* (*an edge, rim, or margin*). Note that a border can also be a line on a map that marks off two different areas, such as states or countries.

Europe

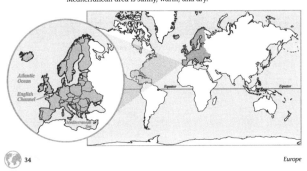

LESSON 6

peninsula   ethnic conflict   service industry   European Union
channel   border   tourism   common currency
ethnic group   manufacturing

Europe includes more than 40 countries and 150 ethnic groups. Read this selection to learn how European countries are working together.

Europe

Lots of Water

Water is in and around Europe. Three large peninsulas form a large part of Europe. A **peninsula** is an area of land that is mostly surrounded by water. It is joined to a larger area of land. Inland waterways provide transportation routes throughout Europe.

Not all of Europe is joined, however. Islands are part of Europe, too. For example, a channel separates Great Britain from the main part of Europe. A **channel** is a narrow sea. It runs between two large areas of land.

Europe has many different climates. The Alps are capped with snow all year. The British Isles are cool and rainy. The Mediterranean area is sunny, warm, and dry.

34   Europe

Many Ethnic Groups

Nearly one-eighth of the world's people live in Europe. Each country is home to one or more ethnic groups. An **ethnic group** is a group of people who have common ancestors, history, language, and way of life.

In the past, Europe saw much **ethnic conflict**, or fighting among ethnic groups. Sometimes after a war, the border between countries changed. A **border** is an imaginary line that separates countries.

Europe Today

Europe today is a mix of old and new. Centuries-old buildings stand next to new factories.

Many countries have a high degree of industrialization. **Manufacturing**, the making of goods by machine, is common in most countries. Farming is still important, too. For example, France grows a lot of wheat.

The service industry is also important. A **service industry** is a group of businesses that provides services. One important service industry is **tourism**. That is the business of helping people travel on vacations. People from all over the world enjoy Europe's fine food, art, and natural beauty.

Many of Europe's countries have formed the **European Union (EU)**. It is a group of countries working together to make better lives for their people.

In 2002, the European Union decided to create a **common currency**. This is a system of money that is shared by different countries. Each country agreed to have the euro as its money. Fewer than 100 years ago, this would have been unthinkable. Then, these countries were at war with one another!

Castles built long ago are found all across Europe.

Chemical manufacturing takes place at this modern European factory.

My World Geography Vocabulary
Go to page 96 to list other words you have learned about Europe.

Europe   35

DURING READING

Read the selection aloud to students as they follow along in their book, pausing at the end of each paragraph or section. Review any words or concepts that students are having trouble understanding. Remind students that there is a glossary at the back of their book that contains all of the words that appear in boldfaced type in the lesson.

- Refer students to the map on page 34. Have students identify a channel, a peninsula, and a border.

- Ask students to name other words in the same word family as *tourism* (*tour, tourist, tour guide*). Discuss how the meaning of each word is related.

- Point out to students that EU is an abbreviation, or short form of a word, for European Union. Ask students what other abbreviations they are familiar with. Students may mention U.S.A., Mr., Mrs., state abbreviations, and others

Have students read the selection again on their own.

AFTER READING

Review Graphic Organizer

Answer any questions students have about the reading selection. Then have students complete or review their graphic organizer and share it with the class.

Summarize

Have students work together to come up with either a written or an oral summary of the lesson. Encourage students to use the target vocabulary words as the basis of their summary. Have students share their summary with the class.

My Social Studies Vocabulary

Encourage students to turn to My Social Studies Vocabulary on page 95 of the student book and use the space provided to add other words about Europe.

peninsula   ethnic conflict   service industry   European Union
channel   border   tourism   common currency
ethnic group   manufacturing

A. Fill in the blanks with the correct vocabulary word.

1. a group of businesses that provides services
   s e r v i c e   i n d u s t r y

2. an imaginary line that separates countries
   b o r d e r

3. the business of helping people travel on vacations
   t o u r i s m

4. the making of goods by machine
   m a n u f a c t u r i n g

5. an area of land that extends from a landmass and is mostly surrounded by water
   p e n i n s u l a

6. a system of money that is shared by different countries
   c o m m o n   c u r r e n c y

7. a group of countries that are working together to make better lives for their people
   E u r o p e a n   U n i o n

8. a group of people who have common ancestors, history, language, and a way of life
   e t h n i c   g r o u p

9. fighting among ethnic groups
   e t h n i c   c o n f l i c t

10. a narrow sea between two large areas of land
    c h a n n e l

36   Europe

---

peninsula   ethnic conflict   service industry   European Union
channel   border   tourism   common currency
ethnic group   manufacturing

B. Circle the word that makes sense in each sentence. Then write the word.

1. People in an (ethnic conflict, (ethnic group)) have many things in common. ___ethnic group___

2. After a war, the (peninsula, (border)) between two countries might change. ___border___

3. Great Britain is separated from the main area of Europe by a ((channel,) common currency). ___channel___

4. Goods are produced by the ((manufacturing,) tourism) industry. ___manufacturing___

5. Countries who are members of the (service industry, (European Union)) are working together toward shared goals. ___European Union___

6. A large area of land that is surrounded by water on most sides is a ((peninsula) channel). ___peninsula___

7. People who are on vacation are served by the (manufacturing, (tourism)) industry. ___tourism___

8. Money looks the same from country to country when the countries share a (border, (common currency)). ___common currency___

9. No goods are produced in a ((service industry,) European Union). ___service industry___

10. When fighting between two groups is based on their ethnic background, that is an (ethnic group, (ethnic conflict)). ___ethnic conflict___

ROOT
The word **ethnic** comes from the Greek word **ethnos**, which means "people" or "nation."

Europe   37

ACTIVITIES A–D

Encourage students to complete as many of the activities as possible. Remind students that they may refer to the Glossary at the back of their book as they complete the activities. Students may work independently, in small groups, or as a class. When students are done, discuss the answers for each activity.

Extensions

These extension ideas allow you to reuse or expand upon the activities. Share them with students who complete the activities before other students, or have students do them for additional practice with target vocabulary words.

A Write the number of syllables in each word or term.

B Choose four target vocabulary words and scramble the letters. Exchange papers with a partner and unscramble each other's words.

WORD ROOT

Have students use what they learned about the Greek word *ethnos* to make a prediction about the meaning of *multiethnic*. Have them look up the word and discuss its meaning.

C Work with a partner to make two lists called "Places on a Map" and "Activities." Write all the target vocabulary words that belong in each list. Discuss why one or more of the target words does not belong in either list.

D Choose three target vocabulary words, such as *tourism, European Union,* and *manufacturing.* Write a sentence using all three words.

38   Europe

peninsula   ethnic conflict   service industry   European Union
channel   border   tourism   common currency
ethnic group   manufacturing

C. Choose the correct vocabulary word to complete each sentence.

1. Water surrounds a _____ peninsula _____ on three sides.

2. A country's _____ border _____ with another country might change after a war.

3. In most European countries, some goods are produced by _____ manufacturing _____

4. People who have the same language, history, ancestors, and way of life are often in the same _____ ethnic group _____ .

5. People who are in a business that does not produce goods are in a _____ service industry _____

6. Improving people's health, wealth, and safety is the goal of the _____ European Union _____

7. The euro is the _____ common currency _____ of some European countries.

8. People who want to get from the mainland of Europe to Great Britain must cross a _____ channel _____ .

9. When two ethnic groups go to war with each other, that's _____ ethnic conflict _____

10. Visitors from other countries are helped by those who work in _____ tourism _____ .

---

peninsula   ethnic conflict   service industry   European Union
channel   border   tourism   common currency
ethnic group   manufacturing

Students' answers will vary.

D. Use each pair of words in a sentence.

1. European Union, tourism
   The European Union is using a common currency, so tourism in member nations might increase.

2. ethnic group, ethnic conflict
   Ethnic conflict might be like gang violence because it's one ethnic group fighting another for control over an area.

3. border, common currency
   If countries have a common currency, the money is the same when you cross countries' borders.

4. peninsula, channel
   A peninsula is land that reaches out into water, but a channel is water between two bodies of land.

5. manufacturing, service industry
   Manufacturing produces goods, but the service industry produces help.

Write!

Write your response to the prompt on a separate sheet of paper. Use as many vocabulary words as you can in your writing.

What do the countries in Europe have in common?

Write!

Provide each student with a copy of Writing Graphic Organizer: Topic Web, Teacher Guide page 83. Tell students to write "Europe" in the top circle of the web. In the lower circles, they should write what the countries of Europe have in common. Write their ideas in the circles of the topic web. Students may add more circles to the web if needed.

Sample Answer

    The countries in Europe are alike in that they have ethnic groups who have been in an area for a long time. Each country has a mix of old and new, too.

    Because of the peninsulas, rivers, and channels, many countries are near water. Countries have both manufacturing and service industries, such as tourism. Those that belong to the European Union have a common currency.

TAKE-HOME ACTIVITY

Assign the Take-Home Activity to students for additional practice with the target vocabulary words. The reproducible Take-Home Activity for Lesson 6 is on page 89 of the Teacher Guide.

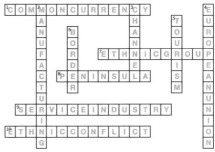

TAKE HOME 6

peninsula   ethnic conflict   service industry   European Union
channel   border   tourism   common currency
ethnic group   manufacturing

Use vocabulary words to complete the puzzle.

Europe

(Crossword puzzle with answers: COMMONCURRENCY, ETHNICGROUP, PENINSULA, SERVICEINDUSTRY, ETHNICCONFLICT)

ACROSS
1 a system of money that is shared by different countries
7 a group of people who have common ancestors, history, language, and way of life
8 an area of land that extends from a landmass and is mostly surrounded by water
9 a group of businesses that provide services
10 fighting among ethnic groups

DOWN
2 the making of goods by machine
3 a narrow sea between two large areas of land
4 a group of countries in Europe that are working together to make better lives for their people
5 the business of helping people travel on vacations
6 an imaginary line that separates countries

Tell someone in your family what you have learned about Europe.

©Curriculum Associates, Inc. *Passwords: Social Studies Vocabulary, World Geography and Cultures, Lesson 6*   89

Europe   39

LESSON 7

Russia

(Student Book pages 40–45)

TARGET VOCABULARY

tundra a flat, bare plain with no trees

permafrost an area of ground that is always frozen

taiga an area of evergreen forests

steppe a dry, flat grassland

communism an economic system in which the government owns all property and businesses

command economy an economy in which the government decides what goods to produce

collective farm a farm owned and managed by the Soviet government

privatization the process of replacing government ownership of businesses with private ownership

consumer good a product that people use

pollution the poisoning of water, land, and air

COGNATES

Spanish-speaking students may find a discussion of similarities and differences between English and Spanish cognates helpful.

English	Spanish
tundra	tundra
permafrost	permafrost
taiga	taiga
steppe	estepa
communism	comunismo
privatization	privatización
pollution	polución

Lesson Summary Russia is the world's largest country in area. In the far north, it is very cold, and there is tundra. South of the tundra is taiga. Russia also has land called the steppe—dry, flat grasslands. Russia has many ethnic groups. It once had a communist government and economic system. At that time, many people lived and worked on collective farms. In the 1980s, privatization began. Soon private companies began producing more consumer goods.

BEFORE READING

Activate Prior Knowledge

Have students fill out a KWL chart about Russia. Tell them to write two things in the first column that they already know about Russia. In the second column, have students write two questions that they have about Russia. Once students have completed the chart, have the class share what they know and want to learn. After students have completed the lesson, they can fill out the last column with things they have learned.

Introduce Target Vocabulary

Tell students that they are about to read a selection about Russia. Write the target vocabulary words on the board. Model the pronunciation of each word and have student volunteers repeat the word. Discuss the meaning of each word and, if necessary, write the definition next to the word.

Present Graphic Organizer

Provide each student with a copy of Vocabulary Graphic Organizer: Word Web, Teacher Guide page 79. Have each student choose a target vocabulary word or assign a word to each student. As students read, they should add information about the target vocabulary word to the graphic organizer.

Word and Definition Cards
for Lesson 7 are on pages 111 and 112
of the Teacher Guide.

VOCABULARY STRATEGY: Word Families

Remind students that they can use the meanings of familiar, related words in the same word family to help them figure out the meanings of unfamiliar words. For example, they may not know the word *collective,* but they can use the word *collect* to help them understand how the Soviet government *collected* small farms together into one big farm and then *collected* the profits from it. Similarly, students may not know the word *privatization,* but they probably know the word *private.* Note that one meaning for *private* is the opposite of *public:* a private owner is often one person, whereas a public owner is often the government or a group. Explain that privatization is the process of returning things to private, or individual, owners.

LESSON 7

tundra   steppe   collective farm   consumer good
permafrost   communism   privatization   pollution
taiga   command economy

Russia is a huge country! However, not many people live there. Read this selection to find out why.

Russia

A Vast, Cold Land

Russia is the world's largest country in area. It stretches across 11 time zones. The Ural Mountains divide European Russia from the main part of Russia.

Much of Russia is cold. In the far north, the climate is subarctic, very cold and frozen. The land here is tundra. A **tundra** is a flat, bare plain with no trees. Snow covers the ground from September through May. A little below the surface, the ground is always frozen. This is called **permafrost**.

South of the tundra is the **taiga**. This is an area of evergreen forests. The ground is not fertile. The climate is cold and windy. There is much snow. South of the taiga are vast steppes. A **steppe** is dry, flat grassland.

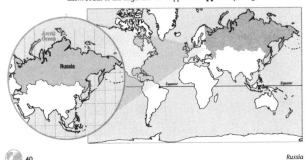

Russia

Many Ethnic Groups

There are many different ethnic groups in Russia. They share a history rich in art, music, and books. Also, they have survived the cold climates and many harsh governments.

Russia Today

After 1917, Russia was called the Soviet Union. It took over many formerly free countries. The Soviet form of government was communism. In **communism**, the government owns all property and businesses. The government decides what goods to produce. This is called a **command economy**.

Every Soviet farm was a **collective farm**. That was a farm that the Soviet government owned and managed. The government gave away the crops as they saw fit. People who worked on collective farms often went hungry.

Under communism, Russians often had to stand in line to buy bread.

By the 1980s, communism had failed. People did not want to work when they were not rewarded for it. The government slowly shifted to a democracy, a government by the people. Privatization soon followed. **Privatization** is the process of replacing government ownership of businesses with private ownership. Soon, businesses began to produce consumer goods that people wanted. A **consumer good** is a product that people use. Consumer goods include clothing and automobiles.

The Soviet Union went back to being Russia. It became a democracy. But people's lives did not change quickly. There are often shortages of goods and services. Many people cannot find jobs.

There is one lasting effect of communism: pollution. **Pollution** is the poisoning of water, land, and air. Careless manufacturing created widespread pollution in Russia.

Pollution from factories has harmed Russia.

My World Geography Vocabulary
Go to page 96 to list other words you have learned about Russia.

DURING READING

Read the selection aloud to students as they follow along in their book, pausing at the end of each paragraph or section. Review any words or concepts that students are having trouble understanding. Remind students that there is a glossary at the back of their book that contains all of the words that appear in boldfaced type in the lesson.

- Make a four-column chart with the headings "See," "Hear," "Smell," and "Touch." Ask students to name things they might *see, hear, smell,* or *touch* if they were visiting the tundra, the taiga, or the steppe. When you are done, review the differences for each type of land.

- Point out to students that the word *permafrost* was created from the words *permanent,* which means "lasting," and *frost.* Discuss with students how this information will help them remember the meaning of the word.

- Write the heading *Communism.* Ask which of these terms belongs under the heading: *command economy, collective farm,* and *privatization.* Have students explain the reasons for their choices.

- Have students give an example of pollution in your town, city, or state.

Have students read the selection again on their own.

AFTER READING

Review Graphic Organizer

Answer any questions students have about the reading selection. Then have students complete or review their graphic organizer and share it with the class.

Summarize

Have students work together to come up with either a written or an oral summary of the lesson. Encourage students to use the target vocabulary words as the basis of their summary. Have students share their summary with the class.

My Social Studies Vocabulary

Encourage students to turn to My Social Studies Vocabulary on page 96 of the student book and use the space provided to add other words about Russia.

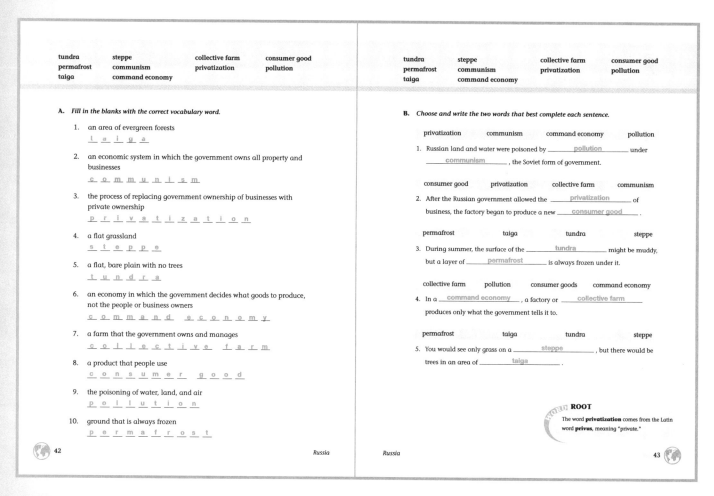

tundra   steppe   collective farm   consumer good
permafrost   communism   privatization   pollution
taiga   command economy

A. Fill in the blanks with the correct vocabulary word.

1. an area of evergreen forests
   t a i g a

2. an economic system in which the government owns all property and businesses
   c o m m u n i s m

3. the process of replacing government ownership of businesses with private ownership
   p r i v a t i z a t i o n

4. a flat grassland
   s t e p p e

5. a flat, bare plain with no trees
   t u n d r a

6. an economy in which the government decides what goods to produce, not the people or business owners
   c o m m a n d   e c o n o m y

7. a farm that the government owns and manages
   c o l l e c t i v e   f a r m

8. a product that people use
   c o n s u m e r   g o o d

9. the poisoning of water, land, and air
   p o l l u t i o n

10. ground that is always frozen
    p e r m a f r o s t

42   *Russia*

---

tundra   steppe   collective farm   consumer good
permafrost   communism   privatization   pollution
taiga   command economy

B. Choose and write the two words that best complete each sentence.

privatization   communism   command economy   pollution

1. Russian land and water were poisoned by _____ pollution _____ under _____ communism _____ , the Soviet form of government.

consumer good   privatization   collective farm   communism

2. After the Russian government allowed the _____ privatization _____ of business, the factory began to produce a new _____ consumer good _____ .

permafrost   taiga   tundra   steppe

3. During summer, the surface of the _____ tundra _____ might be muddy, but a layer of _____ permafrost _____ is always frozen under it.

collective farm   pollution   consumer goods   command economy

4. In a _____ command economy _____ , a factory or _____ collective farm _____ produces only what the government tells it to.

permafrost   taiga   tundra   steppe

5. You would see only grass on a _____ steppe _____ , but there would be trees in an area of _____ taiga _____ .

ROOT
The word **privatization** comes from the Latin word **privus**, meaning "private."

Russia   43

ACTIVITIES A–D

Encourage students to complete as many of the activities as possible. Remind students that they may refer to the Glossary at the back of their book as they complete the activities. Students may work independently, in small groups, or as a class. When students are done, discuss the answers for each activity.

Extensions

These extension ideas allow you to reuse or expand upon the activities. Share them with students who complete the activities before other students, or have students do them for additional practice with target vocabulary words.

A Write a complete sentence by adding the correct answer and a verb to each definition.

B Make a three-column chart. Label the headings "Places," Ideas," and "Things." Write each target word in the correct category.

C Draw a diagram showing how any two target words are related. For example, you might use a diagram to show how a consumer good is related to a command economy.

D Combine any two of the sentences you wrote into a single sentence. Cut or add words so that your new sentence makes sense.

tundra	steppe	collective farm	consumer good
permafrost	communism	privatization	pollution
taiga	command economy		

C. *Choose the correct vocabulary word to complete each sentence.*

1. The cold, windy area of Russia that is covered with forest is the ____taiga____ .

2. People's needs and wants for goods are not considered in a ____command economy____ .

3. The part of the ground that is always frozen is ____permafrost____ .

4. The people who worked on a ____collective farm____ did not get to keep the crops they grew.

5. If you were on a vast grassland in Russia, you would be on a ____steppe____ .

6. During the days of the Soviet Union, the form of government was ____communism____ .

7. After the Soviet Union broke up, the ____privatization____ of business led to making goods that people wanted.

8. The flat, bare land that is the farthest north in Russia is ____tundra____ .

9. A television is an example of a ____consumer good____ .

10. Russia's lakes and rivers continue to suffer from ____pollution____ .

 44   *Russia*

---

tundra	steppe	collective farm	consumer good
permafrost	communism	privatization	pollution
taiga	command economy		

Students' answers will vary.

D. *Use each word in a sentence that shows you understand the meaning of the word.*

1. taiga ____The taiga is a cold, evergreen forest area in northern Russia.____

2. steppe ____Because it is dry, a steppe is not very good for farming.____

3. tundra ____Crops cannot be grown on the tundra.____

4. pollution ____Pollution poisons the air, water, and land.____

5. permafrost ____Plants' roots hit frozen ground in the permafrost.____

6. communism ____No one would get rich under communism.____

7. privatization ____Privatization encourages people to work hard.____

8. collective farm ____There is no reward for hard work on a collective farm.____

9. consumer good ____I am saving money to buy a consumer good.____

10. command economy ____The goods people want are not always available in a command economy.____

 Write!

Write your response to the prompt on a separate sheet of paper. Use as many vocabulary words as you can in your writing.

What are some challenges that people in Russia have had to face?

Russia   45

Write! ✏️

Provide each student with a copy of Writing Graphic Organizer: Cause and Effect Chart, Teacher Guide page 80. Tell students to use the Cause boxes to list challenges, such as the cold climate and Communism. Ask them to use the Effect boxes to write about the responses to and results of these challenges.

Sample Answer

The Russian people have many challenges. The tundra, taiga, and steppes are cold and not good for farming. Their government under communism created a command economy that did not produce the consumer goods that people wanted. People who worked on collective farms did not get rewarded for hard work. After communism collapsed, privatization created privately owned business. However, the country was in such bad shape, things have not gotten better fast.

TAKE-HOME ACTIVITY 📖 ✏️ 🗣️

Assign the Take-Home Activity to students for additional practice with the target vocabulary words. The reproducible Take-Home Activity for Lesson 7 is on page 90 of the Teacher Guide.

TAKE HOME 7

tundra	steppe	collective farm	consumer good
permafrost	communism	privatization	pollution
taiga	command economy		

Use vocabulary words to complete the puzzle.

Russia

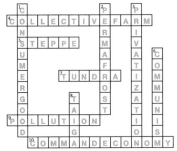

ACROSS

4 a farm that the Soviet government owned and managed

5 a dry, flat grassland

7 a flat, bare plain with no trees

9 the poisoning of water, land, and air

10 an economy in which the government decides what to produce

DOWN

1 a product that people use

2 ground that is always frozen

3 the process of replacing government ownership of businesses with private ownership

6 an economic system in which the government owns all property and businesses

8 an area of evergreen forests

 Tell someone in your family what you have learned about Russia.

©Curriculum Associates, Inc. *Passwords: Social Studies Vocabulary, World Geography and Cultures, Lesson 7*

LESSON 8
North Africa and Southwest Asia

(Student Book pages 46–51)

TARGET VOCABULARY

desert a sandy or rocky area with little or no rainfall

oasis an area in a desert that has water underground

overgrazing allowing animals to eat grass faster than grass can grow back

arable suitable for use as farmland

nationalism strong pride in and loyalty to one's own country

Islam a religion based on the teachings of Muhammad

mosque a place of worship for Muslims

theocracy a government ruled by a religious leader

petroleum an oily liquid that people burn

supply and demand an economic concept that states that the price of a good rises or falls depending on how many people want it and on how much of the good is available

COGNATES

Spanish-speaking students may find a discussion of the similarities and differences between English and Spanish cognates helpful.

English	Spanish
desert	desierto
oasis	oasis
arable	arable
nationalism	nacionalismo
Islam	islam
mosque	mezquita
theocracy	teocracía
petroleum	petróleo

Lesson Summary Much of North Africa and Southwest Asia is desert. The Sahara in North Africa is getting bigger because of overgrazing. Desert peoples come from many different ethnic groups, and nationalism has developed as countries have formed. Most people follow Islam. They worship at mosques. Some governments in the region are theocracies. Many countries in this region are rich in petroleum. Its price rises and falls based on supply and demand.

BEFORE READING

Activate Prior Knowledge

Write the selection title, "North Africa and Southeast Asia" on the board. Under it, write these headings from the reading in a four-column chart: "Desert Lands," "People with a Desert Past," "Followers of Islam," and "Riches from Oil." Invite students to make a prediction about what is covered under each heading. Then invite them to predict which vocabulary words fall under each heading. Record their predictions. Revisit and discuss their predictions after reading.

Introduce Target Vocabulary

Tell students that they are about to read a selection about North Africa and Southwest Asia. Write the target vocabulary words on the board. Model the pronunciation of each word and have student volunteers repeat the word. Discuss the meaning of each word and, if necessary, write the definition next to the word.

Present Graphic Organizer

Provide each student with a copy of Vocabulary Graphic Organizer: Vocabulary Map, Teacher Guide page 78. Have each student choose a target vocabulary word or assign a word to each student. Tell students to write their word in the center box. As they read, students should complete the graphic organizer.

Word and Definition Cards
for Lesson 8 are on pages 113 and 114
of the Teacher Guide.

VOCABULARY STRATEGY: Maps and Diagrams

Encourage students to use both the maps and diagrams to help them understand their reading and to figure out the meanings of unfamiliar words. Note how the maps in each lesson help students understand the region and cultures under study. Refer students to the diagram of supply and demand on page 47. Discuss with students how the diagram helps them understand supply and demand.

LESSON 8

desert   overgrazing   nationalism   mosque   petroleum
oasis   arable   Islam   theocracy   supply and demand

North Africa and Southwest Asia (also called the Middle East) have much in common. Read this selection to find out how they are alike.

North Africa and Southwest Asia

Desert Lands

Much of North Africa and Southwest Asia is hot, dry desert. A **desert** is a sandy or rocky area with little or no rainfall. No grass, bushes, or trees grow there. The Sahara, a desert in North Africa, is almost as large as the United States. It does have some areas of greenery, however. An **oasis** is an area in the desert that has water from underground.

Deserts can happen naturally. Or they can be made by people. **Overgrazing** is the practice of allowing animals to graze, or eat, grass faster than it can grow back. All the plants die. Loose soil blows around in the wind. The land then becomes a desert.

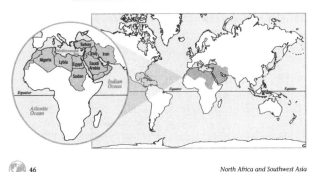

Egypt has the most productive farms in North Africa. But, after overgrazing, less than 5 percent of the land is arable. Land that is **arable** is suitable for use as farmland.

People with a Desert Past

For centuries, various ethnic groups lived in or near the desert. They tended flocks of sheep and herded them from place to place.

More recently, ethnic groups formed countries. Their group loyalty and pride was carried over to the countries in which they live. **Nationalism** is a strong pride in and loyalty to one's nation.

Followers of Islam

Most people here are followers of Islam. **Islam** is a religion based on the teachings of Muhammad. Muhammad taught a belief in one god. Believers in Islam are called Muslims. Muslims pray in a building of worship called a **mosque**.

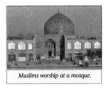

Muslims worship at a mosque.

Some governments in Muslim countries are theocracies. A **theocracy** is a government ruled by a religious leader.

Riches from Oil

Most countries in North Africa are poor. By contrast, most of Southwest Asia is rich. Countries there have vast fields of petroleum under the ground. **Petroleum** is an oily liquid that people burn to create energy. It is the area's greatest natural resource.

This oil field is in Saudi Arabia.

The world depends on oil as an energy source. The oil supply, the amount available, is limited. The demand, the amount people want, is high. **Supply and demand** is an economic concept. It states that the price of a good rises or falls, depending on how many people want it and on how much of the good is available.

My World Geography Vocabulary
Go to page 96 to list other words you have learned about North Africa and Southwest Asia.

46   North Africa and Southwest Asia   North Africa and Southwest Asia   47

DURING READING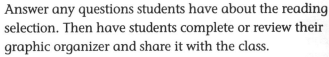

Read the selection aloud to students as they follow along in their book, pausing at the end of each paragraph or section. Review any words or concepts that students are having trouble understanding. Remind students that there is a glossary at the back of their book that contains all of the words that appear in boldfaced type in the lesson.

- Write the terms *desert* and *oasis* in the heads of a two-column chart. Invite students to offer contrasts. Ask which place is arable, and write the word *arable* under *oasis*. Ask which place can be enlarged by overgrazing, and write *overgrazing* under *desert*.

- Ask students to identify the place that fills them, or might fill them, with feelings of nationalism. Ask how they might show their nationalism (*by saluting the flag or collecting items to send to troops*).

- Ask students to draw a sketch or diagram that shows supply or demand for petroleum. Discuss what their pictures, which might illustrate a gas station, traffic, or other uses of petroleum, show.

Have students read the selection again on their own.

AFTER READING

Review Graphic Organizer

Answer any questions students have about the reading selection. Then have students complete or review their graphic organizer and share it with the class.

Summarize

Have students work together to come up with either a written or an oral summary of the lesson. Encourage students to use the target vocabulary words as the basis of their summary. Have students share their summary with the class.

My Social Studies Vocabulary

Encourage students to turn to My Social Studies Vocabulary on page 96 of the student book and use the space provided to add other words about North Africa and Southwest Asia.

North Africa and Southwest Asia   45

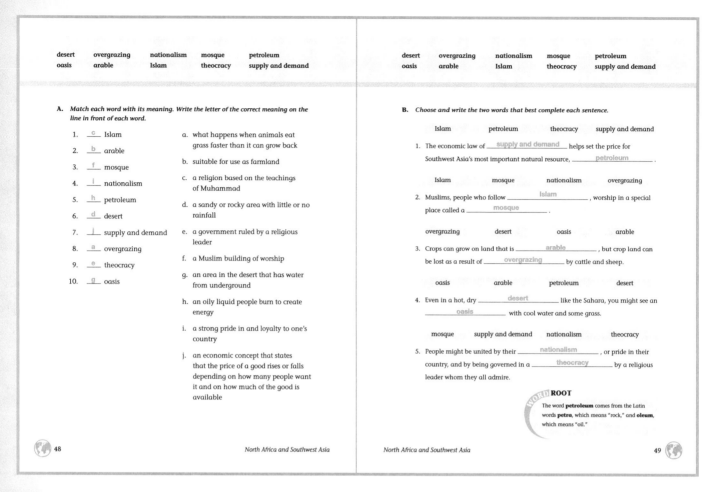

desert   overgrazing   nationalism   mosque   petroleum
oasis   arable   Islam   theocracy   supply and demand

A. *Match each word with its meaning. Write the letter of the correct meaning on the line in front of each word.*

1. __c__ Islam
2. __b__ arable
3. __f__ mosque
4. __i__ nationalism
5. __h__ petroleum
6. __d__ desert
7. __j__ supply and demand
8. __a__ overgrazing
9. __e__ theocracy
10. __g__ oasis

a. what happens when animals eat grass faster than it can grow back
b. suitable for use as farmland
c. a religion based on the teachings of Muhammad
d. a sandy or rocky area with little or no rainfall
e. a government ruled by a religious leader
f. a Muslim building of worship
g. an area in the desert that has water from underground
h. an oily liquid people burn to create energy
i. a strong pride in and loyalty to one's country
j. an economic concept that states that the price of a good rises or falls depending on how many people want it and on how much of the good is available

48   *North Africa and Southwest Asia*

desert   overgrazing   nationalism   mosque   petroleum
oasis   arable   Islam   theocracy   supply and demand

B. *Choose and write the two words that best complete each sentence.*

Islam   petroleum   theocracy   supply and demand

1. The economic law of __supply and demand__ helps set the price for Southwest Asia's most important natural resource, __petroleum__ .

Islam   mosque   nationalism   overgrazing

2. Muslims, people who follow __Islam__ , worship in a special place called a __mosque__ .

overgrazing   desert   oasis   arable

3. Crops can grow on land that is __arable__ , but crop land can be lost as a result of __overgrazing__ by cattle and sheep.

oasis   arable   petroleum   desert

4. Even in a hot, dry __desert__ like the Sahara, you might see an __oasis__ with cool water and some grass.

mosque   supply and demand   nationalism   theocracy

5. People might be united by their __nationalism__ , or pride in their country, and by being governed in a __theocracy__ by a religious leader whom they all admire.

ROOT

The word **petroleum** comes from the Latin words **petra**, which means "rock," and **oleum**, which means "oil."

North Africa and Southwest Asia   49

ACTIVITIES A–D

Encourage students to complete as many of the activities as possible. Remind students that they may refer to the Glossary at the back of their book as they complete the activities. Students may work independently, in small groups, or as a class. When students are done, discuss the answers for each activity.

Extensions

These extension ideas allow you to reuse or expand upon the activities. Share them with students who complete the activities before other students, or have students do them for additional practice with target vocabulary words.

A   Put the target vocabulary words in alphabetical order.

B   Choose one vocabulary word and look it up in a dictionary. Write the word's other meanings or related words.

C   Make a four-column chart with the headings "Land," "People," "Government," and "Economy." Sort the target words into the correct columns.

D   Rewrite your sentences, but leave blanks for the vocabulary words. Exchange papers with a partner, and see if you both can fill in the correct words missing from each other's sentences.

WORD ROOT

Explain that petroleum is found in grains of rock such as sandstone and limestone and that British people refer to gasoline, an oil byproduct, as petrol. Write the word *petrify* and invite students to use their dictionaries to find a meaning of the word that is related to rock.

C. *Write the vocabulary word that best completes each pair of sentences.*

1. A farmer can plant a crop on _____ arable _____ land.

   There is not much _____ arable _____ land in Southwest Asia.

2. Many people in North Africa are believers in the religion of _____ Islam _____.

   Muslims have _____ Islam _____ as their religion.

3. A religious leader is also the head of government in a _____ theocracy _____.

   You might find a government by _____ theocracy _____ in Southwest Asia.

4. Land turns to desert as a result of _____ overgrazing _____ by sheep.

   Keeping sheep in just one area causes _____ overgrazing _____.

5. Southwest Asia's main natural resource is _____ petroleum _____.

   Oil is a word often used to mean _____ petroleum _____.

6. Animals can drink water at an _____ oasis _____.

   You might find plants growing at an _____ oasis _____.

7. The availability of and desire for a good is _____ supply and demand _____.

   The price of a scarce resource goes up because of _____ supply and demand _____.

8. Having pride in one's country is _____ nationalism _____.

   Feelings of _____ nationalism _____ are common in Southwest Asia.

9. Muslims pray in a _____ mosque _____.

   A believer in Islam goes to a _____ mosque _____.

10. You might describe a _____ desert _____ as "hot, dry, and sandy."

    There are no trees in a _____ desert _____.

 50   North Africa and Southwest Asia

Students' answers will vary.

D. *Use each word in a sentence that shows you understand the meaning of each word.*

1. overgrazing ___Overgrazing kills grass because it doesn't have a chance to grow back.___

2. Islam ___Islam is based on the teachings of Muhammad.___

3. desert ___A land that is desert is bare.___

4. mosque ___A mosque is a place of worship for Muslims.___

5. petroleum ___Petroleum, a form of oil, has made some countries rich.___

6. nationalism ___Nationalism is like patriotism.___

7. arable ___Desert land is not arable.___

8. supply and demand ___Supply and demand determines a good's market price.___

9. theocracy ___There is no separation of church and state in a theocracy.___

10. oasis ___A person crossing the desert on a camel would want to find an oasis.___

Write!

Write your response to the prompt on a separate sheet of paper. Use as many vocabulary words as you can in your writing.

What makes North Africa and Southwest Asia different from other regions?

North Africa and Southwest Asia   51

Write!

Provide each student with a copy of Writing Graphic Organizer: Main Idea and Details, Teacher Guide page 81. Tell students to write two or more ideas about the land, people, government, or economy of the region in the main idea boxes. Ask them to use the details boxes to write details that support or explain their main ideas.

Sample Answer

North Africa and Southwest Asia are special because their lands are mostly desert and not arable. Overgrazing has turned some grassland into desert. However, many countries are rich from selling petroleum to other countries. Supply and demand has allowed them to make great profits.

These areas are also special in that many people are followers of Islam and pray in mosques. Some countries in the region are ruled by a form of government known as theocracy.

TAKE-HOME ACTIVITY

Assign the Take-Home Activity to students for additional practice with the target vocabulary words. The reproducible Take-Home Activity for Lesson 8 is on page 91 of the Teacher Guide.

TAKE HOME 8

| desert | overgrazing | nationalism | mosque | petroleum |
| oasis | arable | Islam | theocracy | supply and demand |

Use vocabulary words to complete the puzzle.

North Africa and Southwest Asia

ACROSS

3 a Muslim building of worship

7 suitable for use as farmland

8 a religion based on the teachings of Muhammad

9 a sandy or rocky area with little or no rainfall

10 an economic concept that states that the price of a good rises or falls depending on how many people want it and on how much of the good is available

DOWN

1 an oily liquid that people burn to create energy

2 a strong pride in and loyalty to one's country

4 what happens when animals eat grass faster than it can grow back

5 a government ruled by a religious leader

6 an area in a desert that has water underground

 Tell someone in your family what you have learned about North Africa and Southwest Asia.

91

North Africa and Southwest Asia   **47**

LESSON 9

Africa South of the Sahara

(Student Book pages 52–57)

TARGET VOCABULARY

drought a long period of time without rain

savanna flat grassland with few trees and shrubs

endangered in danger of disappearing from Earth forever

rift a broad, steep-walled valley

subsistence farming growing only enough crops to provide for one's basic food needs

illiterate unable to read and write

overpopulation having more people in an area than the resources can support

famine a serious shortage of food that causes people to die

life expectancy the number of years that people are expected to live

clan a group of people who are related

COGNATES

Spanish-speaking students may find a discussion of the similarities and differences between English and Spanish cognates helpful.

English	Spanish
savanna	sabana
illiterate	iliterato
overpopulation	superpoblación
clan	clan

Lesson Summary Much of Africa is desert. Some of this desert is the result of recent droughts and overgrazing. Africa also has tropical areas. East Africa is a huge savanna. Many animals live there, including endangered animals. Africa is home to the Great Rift Valley, a broad valley with steep walls. Many Africans are illiterate and barely get by on subsistence farming. Overpopulation and famine are great problems of the region. Life expectancy is low. Many people live in extended families and are loyal to their clan.

BEFORE READING

Activate Prior Knowledge

Ask students to think of movies or TV programs about Africa. Ask students to describe the land. Then ask them to describe the lives of the people who live there. Write students' responses on the board. Return to their responses after they have completed the lesson. Have students correct their misconceptions and add to their lists.

Introduce Target Vocabulary

Tell students that they are about to read a selection about Africa south of the Sahara. Write the target vocabulary words on the board. Model the pronunciation of each word and have student volunteers repeat the word. Discuss the meaning of each word and, if necessary, write the definition next to the word.

Present Graphic Organizer

Provide each student with a copy of Vocabulary Graphic Organizer: What Is It Like? Teacher Guide page 77. Have each student choose a target vocabulary word or assign a target word to each student. As students read, they should add information to the graphic organizer.

Word and Definition Cards
for Lesson 9 are on pages 115 and 116
of the Teacher Guide.

VOCABULARY STRATEGY: Prefixes

Remind students that a prefix is a group of letters that appears at the beginning of a word and that changes the meaning of the base word or root word in some way. Write the prefix *il-* and explain that it means "not." Ask students to find the target word that begins with the prefix *il-* (*illiterate*), and explain that *illiterate* means "not literate" or "not able to read and write." Note that there are variations of the prefix *il-*, and write each one: *im-*, *in-*, and *ir-*. Give examples of words that have these prefixes, and have students relate each word's meaning to the meaning "not": *illegal, impossible, inaccurate,* and *irreplaceable.* Encourage students to add these prefixes to the prefix chart on page 100 of their book.

The student book spread:

drought   rift   overpopulation   life expectancy
savanna   subsistence farming   famine   clan
endangered   illiterate

The land south of the Sahara, the world's largest desert, is called Sub-Saharan Africa. Read this selection to find out about the problems this area faces.

Africa South of the Sahara

Vast Land

Much of Africa is desert or near desert. Deserts can develop naturally. They can be created by **drought**, a long time without rain. But people can also cause deserts to spread, too. Poor farming practices have led to more desert land in this area.

East Africa has a vast savanna. A **savanna** is flat grassland. It has few trees and shrubs. Animals, such as lions and elephants, live on the savanna. Many animals are **endangered**. That means that there are so few of them, they may soon disappear forever. Pollution, development, and farming are destroying the animals' habitats.

One of Africa's most unusual landforms is the Great Rift Valley. A **rift** is a broad, steep-walled valley. It is a crack in Earth's crust. It is caused by forces beneath the surface. The Great Rift Valley is 4,000 miles long. It is 6,000 feet deep.

Lakes form as parts of the Great Rift Valley fill with water.

Poor People

Most Africans live in villages. Subsistence farming is common. **Subsistence farming** is growing only enough crops to provide for one's basic food needs. Most people are poor. Many are also **illiterate**. This means they are unable to read and write.

Each year, many Africans leave their villages and move to cities. They come looking for jobs and better opportunities. But life in African cities can be hard. Often there is not enough water, power, or housing.

Many Africans have moved away from villages such as this one.

Overpopulation is a problem everywhere. **Overpopulation** is having more people in an area than the resources can support. Some countries have famines. A **famine** is a serious food shortage that causes people to die.

Overpopulation has led to overcrowded cities.

An African's life expectancy is not as long as that for people in other places. **Life expectancy** is how long people are expected to live.

Ethnic Groups and Clans

In all of Africa, there are about 1,000 ethnic groups. In Nigeria, for example, there are more than 200 ethnic groups. Each ethnic group is made up of clans. A **clan** is a group of people who are related.

Many people view their clan as an extended family. Clans provide people with a sense of security and belonging. People are sometimes loyal to their clan first and their country second. This can lead to conflict between clans within a country.

 My World Geography Vocabulary
Go to page 96 to list other words you have learned about Africa south of the Sahara.

DURING READING

Read the selection aloud to students as they follow along in their book, pausing at the end of each paragraph or section. Review any words or concepts that students are having trouble understanding. Remind students that there is a glossary at the back of their book that contains all of the words that appear in boldfaced type in the lesson.

- Point out the word *danger* in *endangered*. Ask what danger an endangered animal faces.

- Point out the prefix *sub-* in *subsistence*. Explain that *sub-* means "beneath" or "under." Note that people who subsist live with less than they need for a good life, or beneath a level that would allow them to do more than just survive.

- Ask students to identify the prefix in the word *overpopulation* (*over*). Have students figure out the meaning of the prefix based on their understanding of the word (*above*). Have students name other words that begin with the prefix *over-*. Students may mention *oversleep, overweight, overtime, overdue,* or *overhear.* Encourage students to add this prefix to the prefix chart on page 100 of their book.

Have students read the selection again on their own.

AFTER READING

Review Graphic Organizer

Answer any questions students have about the reading selection. Then have students complete or review their graphic organizer and share it with the class.

Summarize

Have students work together to come up with either a written or an oral summary of the lesson. Encourage students to use the target vocabulary words as the basis of their summary. Have students share their summary with the class.

My Social Studies Vocabulary

Encourage students to turn to My Social Studies Vocabulary on page 96 of the student book and use the space provided to add other words about Africa south of the Sahara.

drought	rift		overpopulation	life expectancy
savanna	subsistence farming		famine	clan
endangered	illiterate			

A. Fill in the blanks with the correct vocabulary word.

1. growing only enough crops to provide for one's basic food needs
   s u b s i s t e n c e f a r m i n g

2. unable to read and write
   i l l i t e r a t e

3. a long time without rain
   d r o u g h t

4. how long people are expected to live
   l i f e e x p e c t a n c y

5. a broad, steep-walled valley
   r i f t

6. a serious food shortage that causes people to die
   f a m i n e

7. close to disappearing forever because there are so few
   e n d a n g e r e d

8. a group of people who are related
   c l a n

9. flat grassland with a few trees and shrubs
   s a v a n n a

10. having more people in an area than the resources can support
    o v e r p o p u l a t i o n

---

drought	rift		overpopulation	life expectancy
savanna	subsistence farming		famine	clan
endangered	illiterate			

B. Circle the word that makes sense in each sentence. Then write the word.

1. Africans are often most loyal to their (clan, famine). _____ clan _____

2. People who can't read are (endangered, illiterate). _____ illiterate _____

3. People may go hungry as a result of (overpopulation, life expectancy). _____ overpopulation _____

4. Animals eat grass on a (rift, savanna). _____ savanna _____

5. Forces beneath Earth caused a (rift, drought). _____ rift _____

6. Crop failure in a large area results in (subsistence farming, famine). _____ famine _____

7. Africans die young and do not have a long (savanna, life expectancy). _____ life expectancy _____

8. Animals that might disappear forever from Earth are (endangered, illiterate). _____ endangered _____

9. A lack of rain causes (clan, drought). _____ drought _____

10. Growing just enough food to live is (subsistence farming, overpopulation). _____ subsistence farming _____

ROOT

The word **famine** comes from the Latin word **fames**, meaning "hunger."

ACTIVITIES A–D

Encourage students to complete as many of the activities as possible. Remind students that they may refer to the Glossary at the back of their book as they complete the activities. Students may work independently, in small groups, or as a class. When students are done, discuss the answers for each activity.

Extensions

These extension ideas allow you to reuse or expand upon the activities. Share them with students who complete the activities before other students, or have students do them for additional practice with target vocabulary words.

A Look up two of the target vocabulary words in the Glossary, in the dictionary, and in an encyclopedia. How are the definitions similar? How are they different?

B After you have chosen the correct answer for each sentence, explain why the wrong answer does not make sense in the sentence.

WORD ROOT

Write and say the word *famished*. Have students look the word up and tell how its meaning is related to the root word *fames*. Challenge students to use the word *famished* in a sentence. Note the difference between being literally famished (*starving to death*) and figuratively famished (*hungry before a meal*).

C Write four target words that have a word part (prefix, suffix, root word, or base word) that is familiar to you. Underline the word part. Next to the word target word, write another word you know with the same word part.

D Choose one of the target vocabulary words and use it to create a poem about the word. Write the word vertically down a sheet of paper, one letter per line. Have that letter serve as the first letter of the first word of that line of the poem.

drought	rift	overpopulation	life expectancy
savanna	subsistence farming	famine	clan
endangered	illiterate		

C. *Choose the correct vocabulary word to complete each sentence.*

1. If you are in a valley with high, steep sides, you might be in
   a _____rift_____ valley.

2. A person who is in a _____clan_____ is related to others
   in the group.

3. When people don't have enough to eat and die, the problem is called
   a _____famine_____.

4. Deserts may spread because of overgrazing, poor farming practices,
   or _____drought_____.

5. If an area's resources are not enough for the people living there, the problem
   is called _____overpopulation_____.

6. Elephants live on a _____savanna_____, a flat grassland.

7. How long a person is expected to live is his or her
   _____life expectancy_____.

8. Education can help those who are _____illiterate_____.

9. People who farm and grow just enough food for their own needs
   are practicing _____subsistence farming_____.

10. Many kinds of African animals are _____endangered_____.

Africa South of the Sahara

---

drought	rift	overpopulation	life expectancy
savanna	subsistence farming	famine	clan
endangered	illiterate		

Students' answers will vary.

D. *Use each pair of words in a sentence.*

1. famine, overpopulation
   Overpopulation can result in a famine if there is not enough food
   for everyone.

2. illiterate, subsistence farming
   Some people who practice subsistence farming are illiterate.

3. clan, life expectancy
   A person's life expectancy might be short if his clan is at war
   with another clan.

4. rift, savanna
   A long rift valley and a grassy savanna are two of Africa's land features.

5. endangered, drought
   If animals are endangered, the few that are left might die in a drought.

Write!
Write your response to the prompt on a separate sheet of paper.
Use as many vocabulary words as you can in your writing.
Describe some of the challenges people in Sub-Saharan Africa face.

Africa South of the Sahara

Write!

Provide each student with a copy of Writing Graphic
Organizer: Cause and Effect Chart, Teacher Guide
page 80. Tell students to write reasons for problems in
Sub-Saharan Africa or challenges in Africa in the
cause boxes. Then have them use the effects boxes to
list results or effects of the problems and challenges.

Sample Answer

*Many people in Africa south of the Sahara have a
hard life. Some are illiterate. They can barely stay alive by
subsistence farming what arable land there is. If there is a
drought, a famine results. Overpopulation and clan
conflicts are other problems.*

TAKE-HOME ACTIVITY

Assign the Take-Home Activity to students for
additional practice with the target vocabulary words.
The reproducible Take-Home Activity for Lesson 9 is
on page 92 of the Teacher Guide.

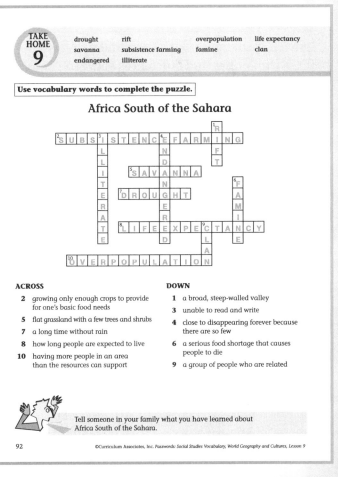

TAKE HOME 9

drought	rift	overpopulation	life expectancy
savanna	subsistence farming	famine	clan
endangered	illiterate		

Use vocabulary words to complete the puzzle.

Africa South of the Sahara

ACROSS
2 growing only enough crops to provide
  for one's basic food needs
5 flat grassland with a few trees and shrubs
7 a long time without rain
8 how long people are expected to live
10 having more people in an area
  than the resources can support

DOWN
1 a broad, steep-walled valley
3 unable to read and write
4 close to disappearing forever because
  there are so few
6 a serious food shortage that causes
  people to die
9 a group of people who are related

Tell someone in your family what you have learned about
Africa South of the Sahara.

©Curriculum Associates, Inc. *Passwords: Social Studies Vocabulary, World Geography and Cultures, Lesson 9*

Africa South of the Sahara

LESSON 10

Central Asia

(Student Book pages 58–63)

TARGET VOCABULARY

landlocked surrounded by land

arid dry

precipitation water that falls to Earth as rain or snow

erosion the washing away of land

earthquake a shaking of part of Earth

tribe a separate family group

nomad a person who travels from place to place

tradition a belief or custom handed down from one generation to the next

Silk Road a trade route that went from China through Central Asia, to the Mediterranean Sea

emigrate to move from one country to live in another

COGNATES

Spanish-speaking students may find a discussion of the similarities and differences between English and Spanish cognates helpful.

English	Spanish
arid	árido
precipitation	precipitación
erosion	erosión
tribe	tribu
nomad	nómada
tradition	tradición
emigrate	emigrar

Lesson Summary Central Asia is landlocked. Much of the land is arid, or dry. Precipitation, which can be heavy when it arrives, often causes erosion. Tribes of nomads have lived in Central Asia for centuries. They have handed down many traditions over hundreds of years. The Silk Road that crossed Central Asia allowed traders to move goods from China to Europe. Today, dry land and water pollution make life difficult in the region. Many people want to emigrate to find better jobs and lives.

BEFORE READING

Activate Prior Knowledge

Direct students' attention to the map on page 58. Pronounce the name of each country included in this region. Discuss with students which of these countries, if any, they are familiar with. Ask students why they might be less familiar with countries in this region than with countries in other parts of the world.

Introduce Target Vocabulary

Tell students that they are about to read a selection about Central Asia. Write the target vocabulary words on the board. Model the pronunciation of each word and have student volunteers repeat the word. Discuss the meaning of each word and, if necessary, write the definition next to the word.

Present Graphic Organizer

Provide each student with a copy of Vocabulary Graphic Organizer: Word Wheel, Teacher Guide page 76. Have students choose a target vocabulary word or assign one to them, and have them write it in the center of the circle. As they read, students should add information about the target vocabulary word to the spokes of the wheel.

Word and Definition Cards
for Lesson 10 are on pages 117 and
118 of the Teacher Guide.

VOCABULARY STRATEGY: Compound Words

Remind students that a compound word is formed by putting two smaller words together. Note that some compound words are closed compounds; that is, the two words make a single word, such as *teammate*. Other compound words are open compounds: the two words make a new term that stands for one thing, such as *home team*. Ask students which target vocabulary words are open or closed compound words (*landlocked*, *earthquake*, and *Silk Road*). Discuss with students how thinking about the small words that make up these longer words can help them figure out or remember the meanings of words.

Central Asia

LESSON 10

landlocked	precipitation	earthquake	nomad	Silk Road
arid	erosion	tribe	tradition	emigrate

The people of Central Asia have lived in that area for centuries. Read this selection to learn about them and their land.

Central Asia

A Dry and Shaken Land

Life in Central Asia is difficult. The area is **landlocked**, surrounded by land. Much of the land is desert or arid grassland. **Arid** means "dry." Other areas get some **precipitation**, water that falls to Earth as rain or snow. However, when it rains, it rains hard. Floods from heavy rain cause erosion. **Erosion** is the wearing away of land by water, wind, or ice.

Earthquakes are common. An **earthquake** is a shaking of part of Earth's surface as a result of underground forces. Earthquakes can kill people and cause much damage.

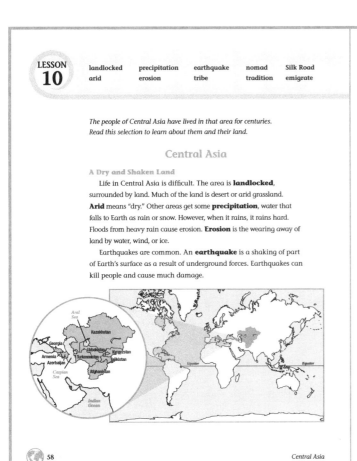

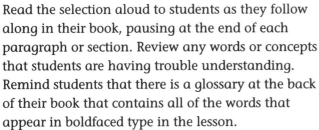

58   *Central Asia*

Desert Tribes

Tribes of nomads have lived in this area for centuries. A **tribe** is a group of people who share a way of life. A **nomad** is a person who travels from place to place in search of food or grazing for animals. People in a tribe share a way of life. Each tribe has its own traditions. A **tradition** is a belief or custom handed down from one generation to the next. For instance, many tribes have worn the same styles and colors of clothing for centuries.

This central Asian nomad wears the traditional clothing of his tribe.

The Silk Road

Beginning about 200 B.C., traders took goods from China to markets in Europe. They traveled across Central Asia on the Silk Road. The **Silk Road** was a trade route that went from China, through Central Asia, to the Mediterranean Sea. It took its name from the most popular trade item, silk. By A.D. 1300, the Silk Road was little used. Sea routes had largely replaced overland trade routes.

Challenges of the Future

The land in Central Asia is dry. The main sources of water are polluted. The Caspian Sea, the world's largest inland body of water, has poor water quality. Its water has been spoiled by spills from oil drilling and untreated waste from sewers and industry. The Aral Sea is also polluted beyond use.

Young people are emigrating to find better jobs and lives. To **emigrate** is to leave a country in order to live in another. Unfortunately, many nations' hopes for the future depend on the young.

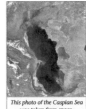

This photo of the Caspian Sea was taken from space.

My World Geography Vocabulary
Go to page 97 to list other words you have learned about Central Asia.

Central Asia   59

DURING READING

Read the selection aloud to students as they follow along in their book, pausing at the end of each paragraph or section. Review any words or concepts that students are having trouble understanding. Remind students that there is a glossary at the back of their book that contains all of the words that appear in boldfaced type in the lesson.

- Ask students to name examples of countries or areas that are not landlocked (*the United States and Canada, Europe, Latin America, Southwest Asia and North Africa*) and explain why they are not landlocked.

- Create a two-column chart on the board. Label the columns "Land" and "People." As students read the selection, have them put the target vocabulary words in the column they think is most appropriate.

- Challenge students to come up with antonyms for these target vocabulary words: *arid, erosion, nomad, tradition, emigrate.*

Have students read the selection again on their own.

AFTER READING

Review Graphic Organizer

Answer any questions students have about the reading selection. Then have students complete or review their graphic organizer and share it with the class.

Summarize

Have students work together to come up with either a written or an oral summary of the lesson. Encourage students to use the target vocabulary words as the basis of their summary. Have students share their summary with the class.

My Social Studies Vocabulary

Encourage students to turn to My Social Studies Vocabulary on page 97 of the student book and use the space provided to add other words about Central Asia.

Central Asia

landlocked   precipitation   earthquake   nomad   Silk Road
arid   erosion   tribe   tradition   emigrate

A. *Fill in the blanks with the correct vocabulary word.*

1. a shaking of part of Earth's surface as a result of underground forces

   e a r t h q u a k e

2. a person who travels from place to place, in search of food or grazing for animals

   n o m a d

3. surrounded by land

   l a n d l o c k e d

4. to leave a country in order to live in another

   e m i g r a t e

5. the wearing away of land

   e r o s i o n

6. water that falls to Earth as rain or snow

   p r e c i p i t a t i o n

7. a belief or custom handed down from one generation to the next

   t r a d i t i o n

8. a trade route that went from China, through Central Asia, to the Mediterranean Sea

   S i l k   R o a d

9. dry

   a r i d

10. a group of people who share a way of life

   t r i b e

---

landlocked   precipitation   earthquake   nomad   Silk Road
arid   erosion   tribe   tradition   emigrate

B. *Choose and write the two words that best complete each sentence.*

    arid   tradition   landlocked   nomad

1. A wandering desert ____nomad____ would never see an ocean because Central Asia is ____landlocked____ .

    precipitation   emigrate   erosion   arid

2. If the land is ____arid____ , it will not get much ____precipitation____ in the form of rain or snow.

    landlocked   erosion   earthquake   tribe

3. The land's surface might be worn down by ____erosion____ or moved by an ____earthquake____ .

    nomad   Silk Road   tribe   precipitation

4. Traders along the ____Silk Road____ might have met a ____tribe____ and exchanged goods with its members.

    tradition   emigrate   earthquake   Silk Road

5. After people ____emigrate____ from their country, they might no longer care about a ____tradition____ they once held dear.

WORD ROOT

The word **nomad** comes from the Greek word **nomas**, which referred to a wandering group of people.

ACTIVITIES A–D

Encourage students to complete as many of the activities as possible. Remind students that they may refer to the Glossary at the back of their book as they complete the activities. Students may work independently, in small groups, or as a class. When students are done, discuss the answers for each activity.

Extensions

These extension ideas allow you to reuse or expand upon the activities. Share them with students who complete the activities before other students, or have students do them for additional practice with target vocabulary words.

A Put the target vocabulary words in alphabetical order.

B Rewrite each sentence as a question.

WORD ROOT

Tell students that another word with the same root is *nomadic*. Have students look the word up, find out its part of speech, and tell how it is related to the root word *nomas*.

C Make a chart with three headings: Nouns (or Naming) Words, Verbs (or Action) Words, and Adjectives (or Describing) Words. Sort the words into the correct column of the chart.

D Choose two of the target words and write a single sentence that uses them both correctly.

landlocked   precipitation   earthquake   nomad   Silk Road
arid   erosion   tribe   tradition emigrate

C. *Choose the correct vocabulary word to complete each sentence.*

1. A trade route called the _____Silk Road_____ once cut across Central Asia.

2. To find grass for his animals, a _____nomad_____ must keep moving from one place to the next.

3. Heavy rain can wash away the soil and cause _____erosion_____ .

4. Some people want to _____emigrate_____ from Central Asia because life there is so hard.

5. It might be a _____tradition_____ for a tribe to welcome strangers with a special meal.

6. Much damage and loss of life can be caused by an _____earthquake_____ .

7. Crops will not grow unless there is warm weather, good soil, and enough _____precipitation_____ .

8. In a _____landlocked_____ country, people cannot meet outsiders in a port city.

9. Many things will not grow in an _____arid_____ climate because of the lack of rain.

10. All the members of the _____tribe_____ spoke the same language.

62   *Central Asia*

Students' answers will vary.
D. *Use each word in a sentence that shows you understand the meaning of each word.*

1. earthquake __An earthquake might cause buildings to fall down.__

2. erosion __Erosion could wash away soil and leave bare rock.__

3. emigrate __The poor family wanted to emigrate to a better land.__

4. arid __Most of the land in Central Asia is arid, so people can't farm.__

5. nomad __A nomad can't own many things because he's always on the move.__

6. landlocked __In a landlocked country, people probably do not eat fresh ocean fish.__

7. precipitation __Some precipitation is good, but too much at once can be a problem.__

8. tribe __All the members of a tribe know one another.__

9. Silk Road __The Silk Road enabled the trade of goods and ideas through many lands.__

10. tradition __Eating turkey is a Thanksgiving tradition.__

Write!
Write your response to the prompt on a separate sheet of paper. Use as many vocabulary words as you can in your writing.
Describe how the land and people of Central Asia are linked.

Central Asia   63

Write!

Provide each student with a copy of Writing Graphic Organizer: Cause and Effect Chart, Teacher Guide page 80. Tell students to use the cause boxes to name the things that affect people's lives. Have them use the effects boxes to name results.

Sample Answer

The land shapes people's lives. Arid land cannot be farmed, and livestock cannot graze long in one place. In areas that do have precipitation, there is a danger that too much will fall. Then erosion might wash away soil and crops. So people became nomads. Perhaps they formed tribes because the land was so harsh, they had to stay together to survive.

In areas where people have settled and built homes, earthquakes can destroy their lives. People either have to put up with the hardships or emigrate.

TAKE-HOME ACTIVITY

Assign the Take-Home Activity to students for additional practice with the target vocabulary words. The reproducible Take-Home Activity for Lesson 10 is on page 93 of the Teacher Guide.

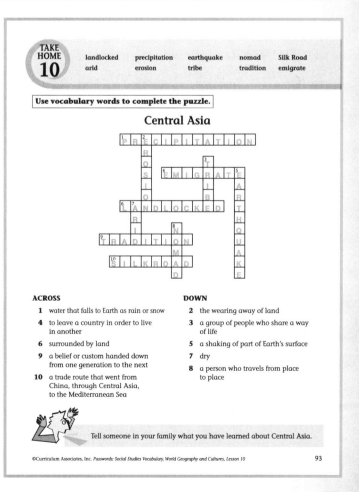

TAKE HOME 10

landlocked   precipitation   earthquake   nomad   Silk Road
arid   erosion   tribe   tradition emigrate

Use vocabulary words to complete the puzzle.

Central Asia

ACROSS
1. water that falls to Earth as rain or snow
4. to leave a country in order to live in another
6. surrounded by land
9. a belief or custom handed down from one generation to the next
10. a trade route that went from China, through Central Asia, to the Mediterranean Sea

DOWN
2. the wearing away of land
3. a group of people who share a way of life
5. a shaking of part of Earth's surface
7. dry
8. a person who travels from place to place

Tell someone in your family what you have learned about Central Asia.

©Curriculum Associates, Inc. *Passwords: Social Studies Vocabulary, World Geography and Cultures, Lesson 10*   93

LESSON 11
South Asia

(Student Book pages 64–69)

TARGET VOCABULARY

subcontinent a large area cut off from the rest of a continent by land features

monsoon a seasonal wind that changes direction twice a year

dialect a different form of the same language

Hinduism a religion based on beliefs in many gods and reincarnation

reincarnation the idea that each soul must be reborn many times

caste a social group into which one is born

Buddhism a religion that teaches that people are too attached to the things of this world

pagoda a tower with many levels

Green Revolution a movement aimed at improving farming methods and crop yields

information technology the use of computer hardware, software, and the Internet to help people process information

COGNATES

Spanish-speaking students may find a discussion of the similarities and differences between English and Spanish cognates helpful.

English	Spanish
subcontinent	subcontinente
monsoon	monzón
dialect	dialecto
reincarnation	reencarnación
caste	casta
pagoda	pagoda

Lesson Summary South Asia is a subcontinent. Its climate varies, but much of India is affected by monsoons. In India, the most popular religion is Hinduism, which is based on beliefs in many gods and in reincarnation. Hinduism also teaches respect for one's caste. Buddhism is the most popular religion in other parts of South Asia. Things are changing in South Asia as the green revolution increases crop yields and information technology spreads through the region.

BEFORE READING

Activate Prior Knowledge

Make a grid with eight boxes. Label them A–C, D–F, G–I, J–L, M–O, P–R, S–V, and W–Z. Then ask students to tell what they know about the climate, landforms, people, religions, and economy of India or South Asia. Record their answers in the grid. After reading, ask students to add other topics and target words to the grid.

Introduce Target Vocabulary

Tell students that they are about to read a selection about South Asia. Write the target vocabulary words on the board. Model the pronunciation of each word and have student volunteers repeat the word. Discuss the meaning of each word and, if necessary, write the definition next to the word.

Present Graphic Organizer

Provide each student with a copy of Vocabulary Graphic Organizer: Word Web, Teacher Guide page 79. Have students choose or assign each student a target vocabulary word. Tell students to write the word in the center circle. As they read, students should add information about their word to the outer circles.

Word and Definition Cards
for Lesson 11 are on pages 119 and
120 of the Teacher Guide.

VOCABULARY STRATEGY: Using Illustrations and Photographs

Remind students that illustrations and photographs, especially in textbooks, can help them understand unfamiliar words by providing a visual explanation or example of them. Point out how the illustrations on pages 64–65 provide meaning and context for some of the target vocabulary words. Encourage students to refer to the illustrations, here and in their other reading, to expand their knowledge of unfamiliar words and to get a better sense of the context as a whole.

LESSON 11

subcontinent	Hinduism	Buddhism	Green Revolution
monsoon	reincarnation	pagoda	information technology
dialect	caste		

South Asia has a rich past and an exciting future. Read this selection to learn about the land and people of South Asia.

South Asia

A Subcontinent

Mountains and deserts cut off South Asia from the rest of Asia. That makes South Asia a subcontinent. A **subcontinent** is a large area cut off from the rest of a continent by land features.

Climate varies across South Asia. Much of India is affected by monsoons. A **monsoon** is a seasonal wind that changes direction twice a year. When the winds blow in from the ocean, they bring rain. When they blow from the land to the ocean, they bring cool, dry weather.

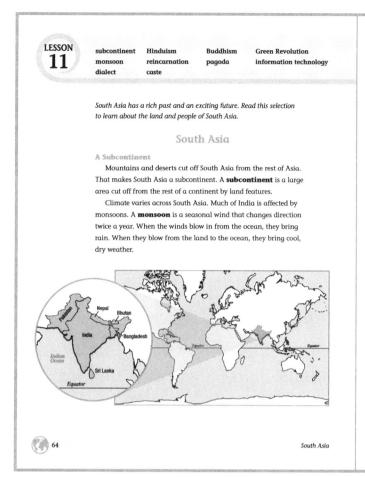

The People

About 16 major languages are spoken in South Asia. But there are hundreds of dialects. A **dialect** is a different form of the same language. Urdu, for example, is the national language of Pakistan. It has at least four different dialects.

The main religion in India is **Hinduism**. A belief in many gods and in reincarnation are central to Hinduism. **Reincarnation** is the idea that each soul must be reborn many times. A person's good deeds in one life may give him or her a better life in the next.

Hinduism also teaches respect for one's caste. A **caste** is a social group one is born into and cannot change. A person's caste determines what jobs and friends a person can have. In Hinduism, people are born into one of four castes. There is also a fifth group— "Untouchables." Hindus once considered them less than human.

Lakshmi is the Hindu goddess of wealth and happiness.

Buddhism is popular in the South Asian countries of Nepal, Sri Lanka, and Bhutan. **Buddhism** is a religion that began in India. Buddhism teaches that people are too attached to the things of this world. Buddhists believe that good deeds will end suffering.

Buddhists practice their teachings in buildings called temples. Some temples are pagodas. A **pagoda** is a tower built with many stories, or levels.

This pagoda is found at a Buddhist temple in Nepal.

Most people in Pakistan and Bangladesh are followers of Islam.

Changing Times

Most people in South Asia live in villages and farm. Many cannot read or write. But more children are getting an education. The Green Revolution has made many lives better. The **Green Revolution** is a movement aimed at improving farming methods and crop yields.

Industry is growing in South Asia. India's fastest-growing industry is **information technology**. It is the use of computer hardware, software, and the Internet to help people to process information.

India is a leader in information technology.

My World Geography Vocabulary
Go to page 97 to list other words you have learned about South Asia.

64   South Asia

South Asia   65

DURING READING

Read the selection aloud to students as they follow along in their book, pausing at the end of each paragraph or section. Review any words or concepts that students are having trouble understanding. Remind students that there is a glossary at the back of their book that contains all of the words that appear in boldfaced type in the lesson.

- Use a classroom map to point out the mountains and the deserts that separate South Asia from the rest of Asia. Review the word *continent* and use the words *continent* and *subcontinent* to identify the different regions. Note that the prefix *sub-* can mean "beneath" or "under," and point out how South Asia appears to be beneath, or below, the rest of Asia when viewed on a map.

- Draw a cause and effect organizer with one cause and two effects. Write the two effects of a monsoon in the effects boxes: rain; and cool, dry weather. Have students name the cause, and record it in the cause box.

- Draw a Venn diagram to compare and contrast the terms *Hinduism* and *Buddhism*. Guide students to include the target words *reincarnation, caste,* and *pagoda* as you complete the diagram together.

Have students read the selection again on their own.

AFTER READING

Review Graphic Organizer

Answer any questions students have about the reading selection. Then have students complete or review their graphic organizer and share it with the class.

Summarize

Have students work together to come up with either a written or an oral summary of the lesson. Encourage students to use the target vocabulary words as the basis of their summary. Have students share their summary with the class.

My Social Studies Vocabulary

Encourage students to turn to My Social Studies Vocabulary on page 97 of the student book and use the space provided to add other words about South Asia.

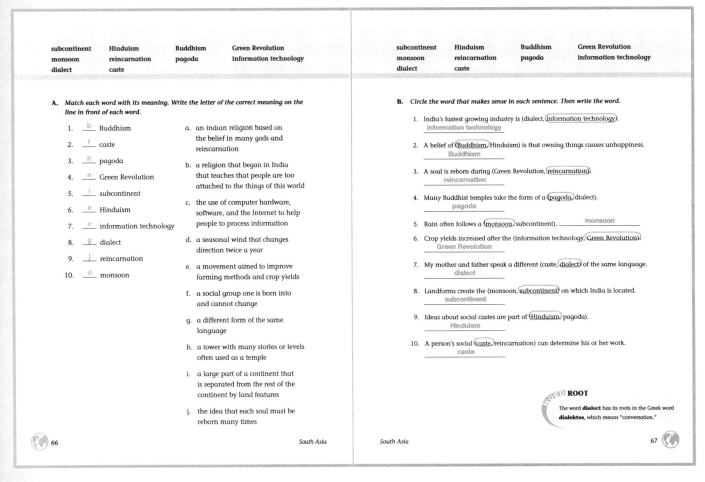

subcontinent   Hinduism   Buddhism   Green Revolution
monsoon   reincarnation   pagoda   information technology
dialect   caste

A. *Match each word with its meaning. Write the letter of the correct meaning on the line in front of each word.*

1. __b__ Buddhism
2. __f__ caste
3. __h__ pagoda
4. __e__ Green Revolution
5. __i__ subcontinent
6. __a__ Hinduism
7. __c__ information technology
8. __g__ dialect
9. __j__ reincarnation
10. __d__ monsoon

a. an Indian religion based on the belief in many gods and reincarnation

b. a religion that began in India that teaches that people are too attached to the things of this world

c. the use of computer hardware, software, and the Internet to help people to process information

d. a seasonal wind that changes direction twice a year

e. a movement aimed to improve farming methods and crop yields

f. a social group one is born into and cannot change

g. a different form of the same language

h. a tower with many stories or levels often used as a temple

i. a large part of a continent that is separated from the rest of the continent by land features

j. the idea that each soul must be reborn many times

66   South Asia

B. *Circle the word that makes sense in each sentence. Then write the word.*

1. India's fastest growing industry is (dialect, information technology).
   information technology

2. A belief of (Buddhism, Hinduism) is that owning things causes unhappiness.
   Buddhism

3. A soul is reborn during (Green Revolution, reincarnation).
   reincarnation

4. Many Buddhist temples take the form of a (pagoda, dialect).
   pagoda

5. Rain often follows a (monsoon, subcontinent).   monsoon

6. Crop yields increased after the (information technology, Green Revolution).
   Green Revolution

7. My mother and father speak a different (caste, dialect) of the same language.
   dialect

8. Landforms create the (monsoon, subcontinent) on which India is located.
   subcontinent

9. Ideas about social castes are part of (Hinduism, pagoda).
   Hinduism

10. A person's social (caste, reincarnation) can determine his or her work.
    caste

ROOT

The word **dialect** has its roots in the Greek word **dialektos**, which means "conversation."

South Asia   67

ACTIVITIES A–D

Encourage students to complete as many of the activities as possible. Remind students that they may refer to the Glossary at the back of their book as they complete the activities. Students may work independently, in small groups, or as a class. When students are done, discuss the answers for each activity.

Extensions

These extension ideas allow you to reuse or expand upon the activities. Share them with students who complete the activities before other students, or have students do them for additional practice with target vocabulary words.

A Put the list of vocabulary words in alphabetical order.

B Draw a picture or diagram to illustrate two of the target vocabulary words.

WORD ROOT

Explain that the Greek prefix *dia-* sometimes means "one with another." Have students relate this meaning to *dialect*. Also, have them relate the meaning of the prefix to the word *dialogue*.

C Do a word chop using the target vocabulary words. Draw a grid of 20 boxes. Divide each target word in half, and write half of each word in a box somewhere in the grid. Exchange grids with a partner, and draw arrows to connect the word parts.

D Many of the target vocabulary words contain smaller words. For example, *Buddhism* includes *bud, him, his, dish, bush,* and *mud*. Make a list of all the smaller words you can find in one target vocabulary word.

subcontinent   Hinduism   Buddhism   Green Revolution
monsoon   reincarnation   pagoda   information technology
dialect   caste

C. *Write the vocabulary word that best completes each pair of sentences.*

1. The most popular religion in India is ____Hinduism____.
   A belief in castes is part of ____Hinduism____.

2. A Buddhist temple may take the form of a ____pagoda____.
   A tower in Asia with many levels might be a ____pagoda____.

3. Farmers were helped by the ____Green Revolution____.
   People had more food after the ____Green Revolution____.

4. Followers of ____Buddhism____ believe good deeds end suffering.
   Many people in Nepal are believers in ____Buddhism____.

5. Landforms that act as barriers create a ____subcontinent____.
   India is a country on the South Asia ____subcontinent____.

6. India's fastest growing industry is ____information technology____.
   Computer hardware, software, and the Internet are part of ____information technology____.

7. Hindus believe that souls are reborn during ____reincarnation____.
   Several different religions believe in ____reincarnation____.

8. A ____dialect____ is a variety of a language.
   A person might speak more than one ____dialect____ of a language.

9. A wind that changes direction is a ____monsoon____.
   A change of season can be brought about by a ____monsoon____.

10. In Hinduism, a person is born into a ____caste____ that cannot change.
    A social group to which a Hindu belongs for life is a ____caste____.

 68   *South Asia*

South Asia   69

subcontinent   Hinduism   Buddhism   Green Revolution
monsoon   reincarnation   pagoda   information technology
dialect   caste

Students' answers will vary.

D. *Use each word in a sentence that shows you understand the meaning of each word.*

1. Green Revolution ____The Green Revolution helped farmers grow better crops.____

2. Buddhism ____Buddhism teaches the value of good deeds.____

3. caste ____A Hindu born into a low caste does not have many options in life.____

4. dialect ____A dialect is not a separate language, just a different version of it.____

5. Hinduism ____Hinduism has many gods and believes in reincarnation.____

6. information technology ____Information technology uses computers to process information.____

7. subcontinent ____India is a subcontinent of Asia.____

8. monsoon ____Monsoons are winds that change the weather.____

9. pagoda ____The pagoda at the temple was five stories high.____

10. reincarnation ____In reincarnation, a person's next life might be better.____

 Write!

Write your response to the prompt on a separate sheet of paper. Use as many vocabulary words as you can in your writing.

How is South Asia different from other places you have read about?

Write!

Provide each student with a copy of Writing Graphic Organizer: Main Idea and Details, Teacher Guide page 81. Tell students to write the main ways in which South Asia is different in the main idea boxes. Then have them use the details boxes to list support or explanation for their ideas.

Sample Answer

South Asia is different in that it is a subcontinent and has monsoons that change the weather. The people have many different religions. Hinduism teaches that there are many gods, people are born into castes, and that souls are reborn during reincarnation. Buddhism teaches that people should detach themselves from owning things and consider the nature of things. Most people in Pakistan and Bangladesh are Muslim.

South Asia is also different in that it combines very old beliefs with information technology and modern farming methods, brought about by the Green Revolution.

TAKE-HOME ACTIVITY

Assign the Take-Home Activity to students for additional practice with the target vocabulary words. The reproducible Take-Home Activity for Lesson 11 is on page 94 of the Teacher Guide.

South Asia

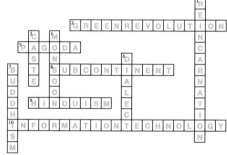

TAKE HOME 11

subcontinent   Hinduism   Buddhism   Green Revolution
monsoon   reincarnation   pagoda   information technology
dialect   caste

Use vocabulary words to complete the puzzle.

South Asia

(crossword puzzle)

ACROSS

2. a movement aimed at improving farming methods and crop yields
5. a tower built on many levels
8. a large area that is cut off from the rest of a continent by land features
9. a religion that believes in many gods and reincarnation
10. the use of computer hardware, software, and the Internet to help people to process information

DOWN

1. the idea that each soul must be reborn many times
3. a social group into which a person is born and cannot change
4. a seasonal wind that changes direction twice a year
6. a different form of the same language
7. a religion that began in India that teaches that people are too attached to the things of this world

Tell someone in your family what you have learned about South Asia.

94   ©Curriculum Associates, Inc. *Passwords: Social Studies Vocabulary, World Geography and Cultures, Lesson 11*

LESSON 12

Southeast Asia

(Student Book pages 70–75)

TARGET VOCABULARY

archipelago a group of islands

inhabited having people living in a place

Ring of Fire an area of volcanic activity along the Pacific Ocean

tsunami a huge sea wave caused by an underwater earthquake

typhoon a violent storm that occurs in the Pacific Ocean

cultivation the act of preparing land and growing crops

paddy a flooded field where rice is grown

terrace farming the growing of crops on step-like levels cut into the soil

port a place where ships can dock

strait a narrow strip of water between large bodies of land

COGNATES

Spanish-speaking students may find a discussion of the similarities and differences between English and Spanish cognates helpful.

English	Spanish
archipelago	archipiélago
inhabited	habitado
tsunami	tsunami
typhoon	tifón
cultivation	cultivación
port	puerto
strait	estrecho

VOCABULARY STRATEGY: Context Clues

Review the context clue signal words that students have already learned for finding definitions as well as the way in which some definitions appear between commas that come immediately after the word. Note that words are also often defined in the next sentence. Point out the term *Ring of Fire* in the first paragraph on page 70. Have students circle the term and underline the definition. Then ask students to find other words in the reading that are defined in the sentence that immediately follows the target word (*tsunami, terrace farming*). Ask them to circle the target words and underline those definitions as well.

Lesson Summary Southeast Asia includes part of mainland Asia and the Malay Archipelago. The islands are part of the Ring of Fire, an area of volcanic activity. The area also experiences earthquakes, which can cause tsunamis, and sometimes has fierce storms called typhoons. Southeast Asia has a warm moist climate, which is perfect for the cultivation of rice. Rice grows in paddies. In hilly areas, people practice terrace farming.

BEFORE READING

Activate Prior Knowledge

Say "Southeast Asia" and ask students to describe the images that come into their mind. Write their descriptions on the board. Then ask students to elaborate on what the land is like and how people live, and record those responses as well. After students have worked through the lesson, return to the board and ask students to correct their misconceptions and add to their lists.

Introduce Target Vocabulary

Tell students that they are about to read a selection about Southeast Asia. Write the target vocabulary words on the board. Model the pronunciation of each word and have student volunteers repeat the word. Discuss the meaning of each word and, if necessary, write the definition next to the word.

Present Graphic Organizer

Provide each student with a copy of Vocabulary Graphic Organizer: What Is It Like? Teacher Guide page 77. Have students choose or assign each student a target vocabulary word. Tell students to write their word in the center box. Students should complete the graphic organizer as they complete the lesson.

Word and Definition Cards
for Lesson 12 are on pages 121 and
122 of the Teacher Guide.

LESSON 12

archipelago   Ring of Fire   typhoon   paddy   port
inhabited   tsunami   cultivation   terrace farming   strait

You probably wear or own more than one thing made in Southeast Asia. Read this selection to learn about the land and people in this area.

Southeast Asia

Extreme Nature

Southeast Asia includes part of mainland Asia and the Malay Archipelago. An **archipelago** is a group of many islands. The country of Indonesia includes about 17,000 islands. Only 6,000 are **inhabited**, or have people living on them. The island area is part of the Ring of Fire. The **Ring of Fire** is an area of volcanic activity along the Pacific Ocean. At least one volcano erupts here every year.

This is also an area of earthquakes. Sometimes they cause a **tsunami**. That is a huge sea wave caused by an underwater earthquake. A tsunami can be 200 feet high and travel as fast as a jet! When a tsunami hits the shore, it causes much damage.

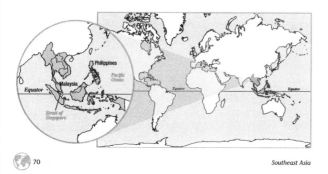

70   *Southeast Asia*

The climate is hot and moist. The rain that comes with seasonal winds floods the area. Typhoons destroy everything in their path. A **typhoon** is a violent storm that occurs in the Pacific Ocean. Wind speeds can reach more than 200 miles per hour!

Cultivating the Land

Most people farm small plots of land. The warm climate and seasonal rains are just right for the cultivation of certain crops. **Cultivation** is the act of preparing land and growing crops. For example, when fields are flooded, people plant rice. In Southeast Asia, rice is grown in paddies. A **paddy** is a flooded field.

In hilly areas, people practice **terrace farming**. That is the growing of crops on step-like levels cut into the soil. When it rains, the terrace prevents the soil from washing away. Many people also have small boats and fish. Some even live on their boats.

Terrace farming allows farmers to catch and use water that flows down hills.

Cities

Foreign countries have factories in Southeast Asia because of the low cost of labor. Cities have grown up around factories. Cities in Southeast Asia are different from those in other parts of the world. Many people get around on bicycles, not cars. The crime rate is low. The streets are clean. Living spaces are very small.

Singapore is the name of both a tiny country and a modern port city. A **port** is a place where ships can dock. Raw materials come into the port. Finished goods from factories leave the port. Ship traffic through the Singapore Strait is brisk. A **strait** is a narrow strip of water between large areas of land.

Many Americans buy goods made in Southeast Asia. The shoes you're wearing might well have been made there!

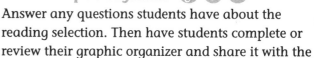
Boats and ships travel down the Singapore Strait.

My World Geography Vocabulary
Go to page 97 to list other words you have learned about Southeast Asia.

Southeast Asia   71

DURING READING

Read the selection aloud to students as they follow along in their book, pausing at the end of each paragraph or section. Review any words or concepts that students are having trouble understanding. Remind students that there is a glossary at the back of their book that contains all of the words that appear in boldfaced type in the lesson.

- Sketch two large landmasses separated by a narrow strip of water. Also, sketch an archipelago. Have students tell which is the strait and which is the archipelago and why. Ask where they might find a port in each of the drawings, and have a volunteer mark one or more spots.

- Ask how the Ring of Fire is related to a tsunami. Develop a word map for *Ring of Fire* and guide students to add concepts related to volcanoes and earthquakes.

- Have students give two examples of cultivation in Southeast Asia (*paddy and terrace farming*). Have them explain the difference between the two types of cultivation.

Have students read the selection again on their own.

AFTER READING

Review Graphic Organizer

Answer any questions students have about the reading selection. Then have students complete or review their graphic organizer and share it with the class.

Summarize

Have students work together to come up with either a written or an oral summary of the lesson. Encourage students to use the target vocabulary words as the basis of their summary. Have students share their summary with the class.

My Social Studies Vocabulary

Encourage students to turn to My Social Studies Vocabulary on page 97 of the student book and use the space provided to add other words about Southeast Asia.

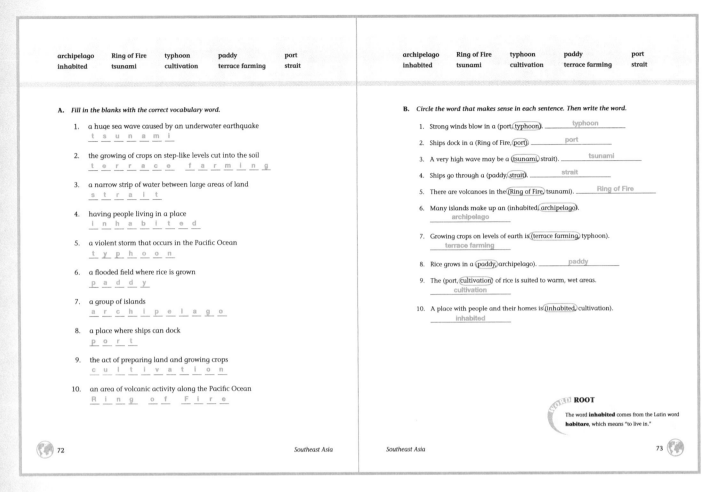

A. *Fill in the blanks with the correct vocabulary word.*

1. a huge sea wave caused by an underwater earthquake
   t s u n a m i

2. the growing of crops on step-like levels cut into the soil
   t e r r a c e   f a r m i n g

3. a narrow strip of water between large areas of land
   s t r a i t

4. having people living in a place
   i n h a b i t e d

5. a violent storm that occurs in the Pacific Ocean
   t y p h o o n

6. a flooded field where rice is grown
   p a d d y

7. a group of islands
   a r c h i p e l a g o

8. a place where ships can dock
   p o r t

9. the act of preparing land and growing crops
   c u l t i v a t i o n

10. an area of volcanic activity along the Pacific Ocean
    R i n g   o f   F i r e

B. *Circle the word that makes sense in each sentence. Then write the word.*

1. Strong winds blow in a (port, typhoon). _____ typhoon
2. Ships dock in a (Ring of Fire, port). _____ port
3. A very high wave may be a (tsunami, strait). _____ tsunami
4. Ships go through a (paddy, strait). _____ strait
5. There are volcanoes in the (Ring of Fire, tsunami). _____ Ring of Fire
6. Many islands make up an (inhabited, archipelago). _____ archipelago
7. Growing crops on levels of earth is (terrace farming, typhoon). _____ terrace farming
8. Rice grows in a (paddy, archipelago). _____ paddy
9. The (port, cultivation) of rice is suited to warm, wet areas. _____ cultivation
10. A place with people and their homes is (inhabited, cultivation). _____ inhabited

ROOT

The word **inhabited** comes from the Latin word **habitare**, which means "to live in."

72   *Southeast Asia*   *Southeast Asia*   73

ACTIVITIES A–D

Encourage students to complete as many of the activities as possible. Remind students that they may refer to the Glossary at the back of their book as they complete the activities. Students may work independently, in small groups, or as a class. When students are done, discuss the answers for each activity.

Extensions

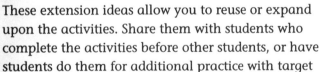

These extension ideas allow you to reuse or expand upon the activities. Share them with students who complete the activities before other students, or have students do them for additional practice with target vocabulary words.

A Write a complete sentence by adding the correct answer and a verb to each definition.

B Choose four target words and scramble the letters. Exchange papers with a partner and unscramble each other's words.

WORD ROOT

Note that *habitation* also comes from *habitare*. Have students look up the word in a dictionary and then state its connection to *inhabited*.

C Renumber the sentences to reflect the order in which the target vocabulary words would appear in a dictionary.

D Circle the nouns and underline the verbs in each sentence you wrote.

C. *Choose the correct vocabulary word to complete each sentence.*

1. Singapore has a _____port_____ where ships can dock.

2. A narrow body of water between two landmasses is a _____strait_____ .

3. A flooded field where rice grows is a _____paddy_____ .

4. Many islands form an _____archipelago_____ .

5. An area along the Pacific with many volcanoes is called the _____Ring of Fire_____ .

6. Growing crops on steps cut into a hillside is _____terrace farming_____ .

7. Rain and warm weather are needed for the _____cultivation_____ of rice.

8. An island with people living on it is _____inhabited_____ .

9. An earthquake under the ocean might cause a _____tsunami_____ .

10. A violent storm in the Pacific Ocean is called a _____typhoon_____ .

Students' answers will vary.

D. *Use each word in a sentence that shows you understand the meaning of each word.*

1. Ring of Fire ___The Ring of Fire would be a good place to see a volcano.___

2. tsunami ___A tsunami is like a wall of fast-moving water.___

3. strait ___Ships travel through a strait.___

4. archipelago ___The archipelago in Southeast Asia has many islands.___

5. port ___Ships bring goods in and out of a port.___

6. inhabited ___Most islands in the Malay Archipelago are not inhabited.___

7. terrace farming ___Terrace farming lets people grow crops on a hillside.___

8. paddy ___Rice grows in a swamp-like paddy.___

9. cultivation ___The cultivation of a crop depends on several factors.___

10. typhoon ___A typhoon is a strong wind.___

Write!
Write your response to the prompt on a separate sheet of paper.
Use as many vocabulary words as you can in your writing.
What is unusual about Southeast Asia?

Write!

Provide each student with a copy of Writing Graphic Organizer: Main Idea and Details Chart, Teacher Guide page 81. Suggest that students work in pairs to write two or three main ideas about what makes Southeast Asia unusual. Then have them list details that support each main idea. Ask students to use the organizer to write their own responses.

Sample Answer

    Southeast Asia is unusual because of its many dangers. An archipelago called the Ring of Fire has volcanoes. Tsunamis and typhoons threaten people's lives.

    The area has clever people, too. They use heavy rains for the cultivation of rice. They use terrace farming to turn hillsides into farmland and to avoid erosion from rain.

    It's surprising that Singapore has such a busy port. It's also surprising that most cities in Southeast Asia are clean, don't have much crime, and have more bicycles than cars.

TAKE-HOME ACTIVITY

Assign the Take-Home Activity to students for additional practice with the target vocabulary words. The reproducible Take-Home Activity for Lesson 12 is on page 95 of the Teacher Guide.

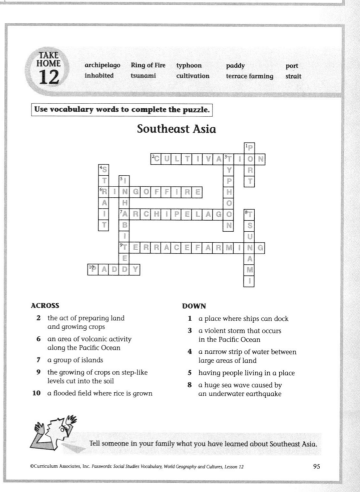

TAKE HOME 12

archipelago   Ring of Fire   typhoon   paddy   port
inhabited   tsunami   cultivation   terrace farming   strait

Use vocabulary words to complete the puzzle.

Southeast Asia

(crossword puzzle with answers: CULTIVATION, RING OF FIRE, ARCHIPELAGO, TERRACE FARMING, PADDY, and down words PORT, STRAIT, TYPHOON, INHABITED, TSUNAMI)

ACROSS

2 the act of preparing land and growing crops

6 an area of volcanic activity along the Pacific Ocean

7 a group of islands

9 the growing of crops on step-like levels cut into the soil

10 a flooded field where rice is grown

DOWN

1 a place where ships can dock

3 a violent storm that occurs in the Pacific Ocean

4 a narrow strip of water between large areas of land

5 having people living in a place

8 a huge sea wave caused by an underwater earthquake

Tell someone in your family what you have learned about Southeast Asia.

95

LESSON 13

East Asia

(Student Book pages 76–81)

Lesson Summary Some island nations developed in isolation. This led to a homogeneous society, like that of Japan. The Japanese express their culture in unique ways. These include a kind of poetry called haiku and artistic writing called calligraphy. They also include a form of theater called kabuki, and traditional forms of fighting and exercise known as the martial arts. Japan and South Korea are now part of the global economy. They depend on other countries for their well-being.

TARGET VOCABULARY

isolation cut off from other areas or people

homogeneous society a society made up mostly of the same kind of people

haiku a traditional Japanese poem with three lines

calligraphy beautiful writing

kabuki a form of Japanese drama

martial arts traditional forms of fighting and exercise

global economy an interdependent world economic system

interdependence relying on others for well-being

trade surplus more exports than imports

trade deficit more imports than exports

COGNATES

Spanish-speaking students may find a discussion of the similarities and differences between English and Spanish cognates helpful.

English	Spanish
isolation	aislamiento
homogeneous society	sociedad homogénea
haiku	haiku
calligraphy	caligrafía
kabuki	kabuki

BEFORE READING

Activate Prior Knowledge

Draw a two-column chart on the board. Write the title "East Asia," and explain that it includes Japan and North and South Korea. Then label the column headings "People and Culture" and "Business and Economics." Ask students to tell what they know about each category. Record their answers in the chart. After reading, review and, as needed, correct the chart.

Introduce Target Vocabulary

Tell students that they are about to read a selection about East Asia. Write the target vocabulary words on the board. Model the pronunciation of each word and have student volunteers repeat the word. Discuss the meaning of each word and, if necessary, write the definition next to the word.

Present Graphic Organizer

Provide each student with a copy of Vocabulary Graphic Organizer: Vocabulary Map, Teacher Guide page 78. Have students choose a target vocabulary word or assign one to them. As they read, students should fill in as many parts of the map as they can.

Word and Definition Cards
for Lesson 13 are on pages 123 and
124 of the Teacher Guide.

VOCABULARY STRATEGY: Antonyms

Review with students the definition of antonyms—words that have opposite or nearly opposite meanings. Have students provide examples of common antonyms, such as *large/small, buy/sell,* and *rich/poor.* Tell students that knowing antonyms can help them increase their vocabulary. Also, antonyms can sometimes be context clues that help show the meaning of a word. Tell students that one pair of target words are antonyms (*trade surplus/trade deficit*). Discuss why they are opposite in meaning.

East Asia

LESSON
13

isolation   calligraphy   global economy   trade surplus
homogeneous society   kabuki   interdependence   trade deficit
haiku   martial arts

The countries in East Asia are different from other Asian countries.
Read this passage to find out about those differences.

East Asia

Isolation

East Asia includes a mainland and islands. Some countries, such as Japan, developed in isolation. **Isolation** means cut off from other areas and people. The Japanese had little contact with outsiders. They developed a **homogeneous society**. That is a society made up of mostly the same kind of people. They look similar and have the same culture.

Japanese Culture

Japanese people value beauty and simplicity in their arts. For example, a **haiku** is a traditional Japanese poem. It is written in three lines. The lines have five, seven, and five syllables. These poems usually focus on nature or the poet's feelings.

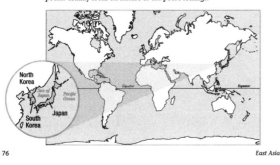

Many Japanese arts have roots in China. **Calligraphy**, the art of beautiful writing, began in China. Japanese artists soon developed their own style. Today, Japanese children study calligraphy in school.

This elementary school student practices calligraphy.

Kabuki is a form of Japanese drama. It combines singing, dancing, bold makeup, and elaborate costumes.

Many Americans have watched movies showing Japanese **martial arts**. They are traditional forms of fighting and exercise that use the hands and feet.

A Global Economy

Japan and South Korea are part of a **global economy**. They trade with many countries. Their economies are based on interdependence. **Interdependence** means that countries rely on and affect each other. If one country has money problems, it affects other countries too.

Until recently, North Korea traded with few other countries. Most of its people are farmers. They were not able to grow enough food to feed everyone. Many North Koreans went hungry.

North Korean farmers lack modern farm machinery.

Countries need to trade goods to keep their economies strong. A **trade surplus** happens when there are more exports than imports. A **trade deficit** happens when there are more imports than exports. Countries must be able to buy goods they need—and have money to pay for them.

South Korea and Japan have a trade surplus with the United States. They export more goods to the United States than they import.

My World Geography Vocabulary
Go to page 98 to list other words you have learned about East Asia.

DURING READING

Read the selection aloud to students as they follow along in their book, pausing at the end of each paragraph or section. Review any words or concepts that students are having trouble understanding. Remind students that there is a glossary at the back of their book that contains all of the words that appear in boldfaced type in the lesson.

- Work with students to list things that might be the same in a homogeneous culture (*language, religion, beliefs, traditions*). Contrast a homogenous culture with the culture of the United States.

- Point out the prefix *inter-* in *interdependent* and explain that it means "between" or "among." Also point out the base word *depend* and the suffix *-ent* which makes the word an adjective. Talk about how the meaning of each word part is related to the whole word.

- Explain that Japan exports more goods to the United States than it imports from the United States. Have students name the term that describes this state of trade (*trade surplus*).

Have students read the selection again on their own.

AFTER READING

Review Graphic Organizer

Answer any questions students have about the reading selection. Then have students complete or review their graphic organizer and share it with the class.

Summarize

Have students work together to come up with either a written or an oral summary of the lesson. Encourage students to use the target vocabulary words as the basis of their summary. Have students share their summary with the class.

My Social Studies Vocabulary

Encourage students to turn to My Social Studies Vocabulary on page 98 of the student book and use the space provided to add other words about East Asia.

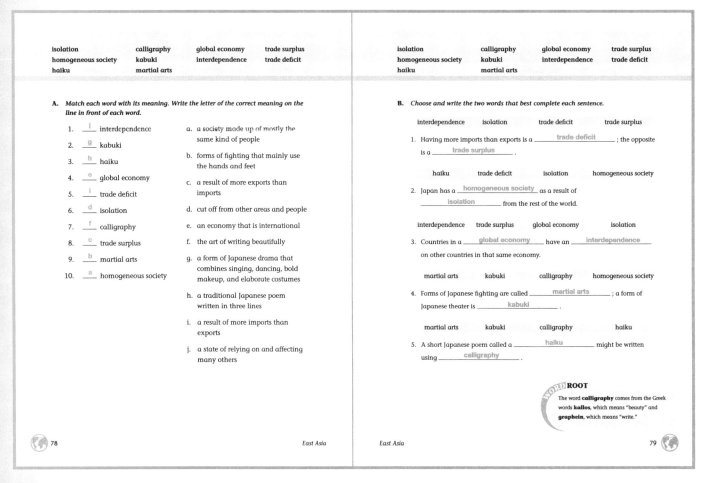

ACTIVITIES A–D

Encourage students to complete as many of the activities as possible. Remind students that they may refer to the Glossary at the back of their book as they complete the activities. Students may work independently, in small groups, or as a class. When students are done, discuss the answers for each activity.

Extensions

These extension ideas allow you to reuse or expand upon the activities. Share them with students who complete the activities before other students, or have students do them for additional practice with target vocabulary words.

A Draw a line between the syllables in each vocabulary word.

B Choose two sentences that were not paired and write a sentence that includes both words.

WORD ROOT

Note to students that other words are related to *graphein*: *graph*, *graphic*, and *autograph*. Ask students to look up the words in a dictionary and then describe the connection.

C Draw a diagram showing how any two target words are related. For example, you might use a diagram to show how one word is an example that fits in a category named by another word.

D Rewrite your sentences, but leave blanks for the vocabulary words. Exchange papers with a partner, and see if you both can fill in the correct words missing from each other's sentences.

isolation	calligraphy	global economy	trade surplus
homogeneous society	kabuki	interdependence	trade deficit
haiku	martial arts		

C. *Choose the correct vocabulary word to complete each sentence.*

1. When more than two countries' economies affect each other, that creates an
   __interdependence__ .

2. A poem that has three lines with five, seven, and five syllables is a
   __haiku__ .

3. A country in __isolation__ has no outside contact.

4. Fancy stage sets are part of __kabuki__ .

5. If Japan sold more goods to other countries than it bought, it would have a
   __trade surplus__ .

6. American movies made __martial arts__ fighting popular.

7. If South Korea bought more goods from other countries than it sold, it would
   have a __trade deficit__ .

8. When people have the same looks and beliefs, they form a
   __homogeneous society__ .

9. A worldwide economy is a __global economy__ .

10. The Japanese create beautiful writing called __calligraphy__
    with a brush and black ink.

---

isolation	calligraphy	global economy	trade surplus
homogeneous society	kabuki	interdependence	trade deficit
haiku	martial arts		

Students' answers will vary.

D. *Use each word in a sentence that shows you understand the meaning of each word.*

1. martial arts __Martial arts use hands and feet as weapons.__

2. kabuki __Kabuki is art and entertainment.__

3. trade surplus __A country that sells more than it buys has__
   __a trade surplus.__

4. calligraphy __Calligraphy is artistic writing.__

5. haiku __A haiku is a three-line poem.__

6. isolation __Island countries often develop in isolation from others.__

7. trade deficit __A country that buys more than it sells has a trade deficit.__

8. interdependence __Countries with economic interdependence must__
   __get along.__

9. homogeneous society __A nation of immigrants can never form a__
   __homogeneous society.__

10. global economy __A global economy results from goods being traded__
    __around the world.__

Write!

Write your response to the prompt on a separate sheet of paper.
Use as many vocabulary words as you can in your writing.

Would you like to visit East Asia? Why or why not?

Write!

Provide each student with a copy of Writing Graphic Organizer: Two-Column Chart, Teacher Guide page 82. Tell students to write these headings: "Reasons to Visit" and "Reasons Not to Visit." Record reasons in each column of the chart, and then decide which ideas you will present in your writing.

Sample Answer

   I would like to visit Japan. It might be interesting to see kabuki, to have my name written in Japanese calligraphy, and to watch real martial arts fighting. Japan and the United States are both part of the world economy. I might feel comfortable there. I wouldn't want to go to North Korea where there is a shortage of food.

TAKE-HOME ACTIVITY

Assign the Take-Home Activity to students for additional practice with the target vocabulary words. The reproducible Take-Home Activity for Lesson 13 is on page 96 of the Teacher Guide.

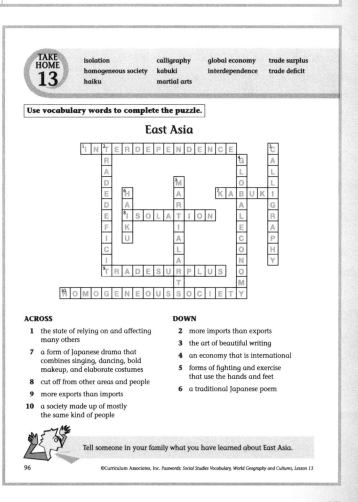

TAKE HOME 13

isolation	calligraphy	global economy	trade surplus
homogeneous society	kabuki	interdependence	trade deficit
haiku	martial arts		

Use vocabulary words to complete the puzzle.

East Asia

ACROSS

1. the state of relying on and affecting many others
7. a form of Japanese drama that combines singing, dancing, bold makeup, and elaborate costumes
8. cut off from other areas and people
9. more exports than imports
10. a society made up of mostly the same kind of people

DOWN

2. more imports than exports
3. the art of beautiful writing
4. an economy that is international
5. forms of fighting and exercise that use the hands and feet
6. a traditional Japanese poem

Tell someone in your family what you have learned about East Asia.

LESSON 14

China

(Student Book pages 82–87)

TARGET VOCABULARY

distribution spread

fossil fuels coal, oil, or natural gas

gorge a canyon with steep walls

reservoir a lake created by a dam

hydroelectricity energy created by water that is allowed to flow over a dam

Confucianism a belief system that stresses the value of family and the duties that people owe one another

Taoism a belief system that stresses finding balance with nature

acid rain rain that carries pollution in the air to the ground

repression the putting down of citizens' human rights

human rights rights that every person should have, including freedom of speech and religion

COGNATES

Spanish-speaking students may find a discussion of the similarities and differences between English and Spanish cognates helpful.

English	Spanish
distribution	distribución
gorge	gorja
Confucianism	confucianismo
Taoism	taoísmo
repression	represión

Lesson Summary One of China's natural resources is the Yangtze River. China is building the Three Gorges Dam to create a huge reservoir from this river. This dam will help China create hydroelectricity and cut down on its use of fossil fuels, especially coal. Most of the people of China are part of the same ethnic group. Many follow the teachings of Confucianism or Taoism. China faces many problems that include acid rain and the repression of human rights.

BEFORE READING

Activate Prior Knowledge

Have students fill out a KWL chart about China. Tell them to write two things in the first column that they already know about China. In the second column, have students write two questions that they have about China. Once students have completed the chart, have the class share what they know and want to learn. Return to the charts when students have completed the lesson so that they can fill out the last column with things they have learned.

Introduce Target Vocabulary

Tell students that they are about to read a selection about China. Write the target vocabulary words on the board. Model the pronunciation of each word and have student volunteers repeat the word. Discuss the meaning of each word and, if necessary, write the definition next to the word.

Present Graphic Organizer

Provide each student with a copy of Vocabulary Graphic Organizer: Word Wheel, Teacher Guide page 76. Have each student choose a target vocabulary word or assign a target word to each student. As students read, they should add information about the target vocabulary word to the graphic organizer.

Word and Definition Cards
for Lesson 14 are on pages 125 and
126 of the Teacher Guide.

VOCABULARY STRATEGY: Suffixes

Write the suffix *-ism* and have students identify the two target words that contain this suffix (*Confucianism* and *Taoism*). Ask students to name words they know with this suffix. Explain that *-ism* is a suffix that means "a set of ideas or a practice."

Note that Confucianism and Taoism are both belief systems, or a set of ideas about ways to live and act. Encourage students to add the suffix *-ism* to the suffix chart on page 100 of their book.

China

distribution   gorge   hydroelectricity   Taoism   repression
fossil fuels   reservoir   Confucianism   acid rain   human rights

China has one of the oldest cultures in the world. Yet it has modern problems. Read this selection to learn about China.

China

Changing the Land

China is the largest country in East Asia. It has mountain ranges, deserts, plateaus, and rivers. It has natural resources, too. However, their **distribution**, or spread, throughout China is not equal.

The 4,000-mile Yangtze River is one natural resource. But it floods often. In the last 100 years, its floods have killed one million people. Another natural resource is coal. China burns about 50 million tons of coal each year. However, supplies of this fossil fuel are limited. **Fossil fuels** include coal, oil, and natural gas. They formed millions of years ago from the remains of living things.

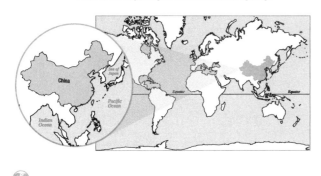

Changing the Land

The government wants to control flooding. It also wants to cut the use of coal. So it built the largest dam in the world. The dam is 1.5 miles wide and 600 feet high. It is called the Three Gorges Dam, after the natural gorges in the area. A **gorge** is a canyon with steep walls.

The dam holds back water from the Yangtze River in a reservoir. A **reservoir** is a lake that people have made to store water. The reservoir is 400 miles long. The dam provides **hydroelectricity**. That is energy created by water allowed to fall over a dam. When the dam is working fully, it will supply one-ninth of China's energy.

More than one million people had to move to make way for the Three Gorges Dam and its reservoir.

People's Beliefs

China is home to more than one billion people. About 94 percent of them belong to the same ethnic group. Many follow **Confucianism**. This belief system stresses the value of family and the duties that people owe each other. Respect for the elderly and education are highly valued.

Many people also follow **Taoism**. This belief system stresses finding inner peace and accepting change.

Followers of Confucianism built this temple in China.

China's Problems

China is working to become modern. In doing so, it has created problems. Burning coal pollutes the air. Then acid rain falls. **Acid rain** is rain that carries pollution in the air to the ground. Acid rain harms plants and crops.

Another problem is government repression. **Repression** is the putting down of citizens' human rights. **Human rights** are rights that every person should have. They include freedom of speech and religion. For years, people who spoke or wrote anything that disagreed with government policy were treated badly. They were put in prison or killed.

My World Geography Vocabulary
Go to page 98 to list other words you have learned about China.

DURING READING

Read the selection aloud to students as they follow along in their book, pausing at the end of each paragraph or section. Review any words or concepts that students are having trouble understanding. Remind students that there is a glossary at the back of their book that contains all of the words that appear in boldfaced type in the lesson.

- Write *coal, oil,* and *natural gas* on the board, and have students name the target vocabulary word that includes them all.

- Point out the prefix *hydro-* in *hydroelectricity,* and explain that it means "water." Ask students if they can think of related words (such as *hydroplane*), or supply some related words and explain how they relate to the meaning "water."

- Have students name some human rights they have. Ask how their lives would change if someone repressed, or if there was repression of, those rights.

Have students read the selection again on their own.

AFTER READING

Review Graphic Organizer

Answer any questions students have about the reading selection. Then have students complete or review their graphic organizer and share it with the class.

Summarize

Have students work together to come up with either a written or an oral summary of the lesson. Encourage students to use the target vocabulary words as the basis of their summary. Have students share their summary with the class.

My Social Studies Vocabulary

Encourage students to turn to My Social Studies Vocabulary on page 98 of the student book and use the space provided to add other words about China.

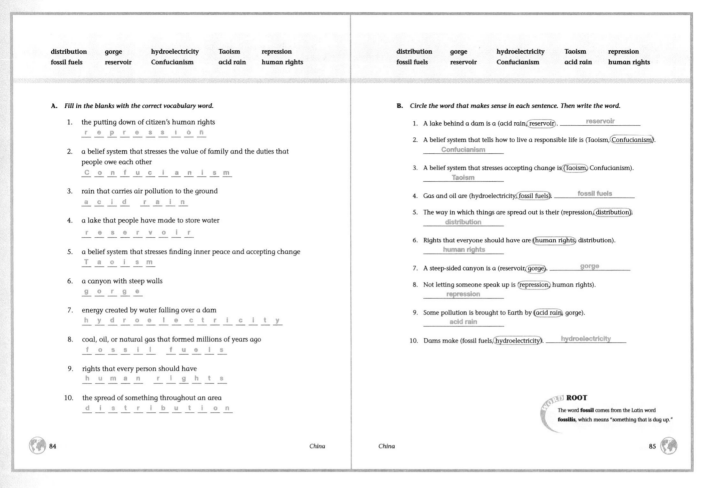

| distribution | gorge | hydroelectricity | Taoism | repression |
| fossil fuels | reservoir | Confucianism | acid rain | human rights |

A. *Fill in the blanks with the correct vocabulary word.*

1. the putting down of citizen's human rights
   r e p r e s s i o n

2. a belief system that stresses the value of family and the duties that people owe each other
   C o n f u c i a n i s m

3. rain that carries air pollution to the ground
   a c i d   r a i n

4. a lake that people have made to store water
   r e s e r v o i r

5. a belief system that stresses finding inner peace and accepting change
   T a o i s m

6. a canyon with steep walls
   g o r g e

7. energy created by water falling over a dam
   h y d r o e l e c t r i c i t y

8. coal, oil, or natural gas that formed millions of years ago
   f o s s i l   f u e l s

9. rights that every person should have
   h u m a n   r i g h t s

10. the spread of something throughout an area
    d i s t r i b u t i o n

84
China

| distribution | gorge | hydroelectricity | Taoism | repression |
| fossil fuels | reservoir | Confucianism | acid rain | human rights |

B. *Circle the word that makes sense in each sentence. Then write the word.*

1. A lake behind a dam is a (acid rain, reservoir). reservoir

2. A belief system that tells how to live a responsible life is (Taoism, Confucianism). Confucianism

3. A belief system that stresses accepting change is (Taoism, Confucianism). Taoism

4. Gas and oil are (hydroelectricity, fossil fuels). fossil fuels

5. The way in which things are spread out is their (repression, distribution). distribution

6. Rights that everyone should have are (human rights, distribution). human rights

7. A steep-sided canyon is a (reservoir, gorge). gorge

8. Not letting someone speak up is (repression, human rights). repression

9. Some pollution is brought to Earth by (acid rain, gorge). acid rain

10. Dams make (fossil fuels, hydroelectricity). hydroelectricity

WORD ROOT
The word **fossil** comes from the Latin word **fossilis**, which means "something that is dug up."

China
85

ACTIVITIES A–D

Encourage students to complete as many of the activities as possible. Remind students that they may refer to the Glossary at the back of their book as they complete the activities. Students may work independently, in small groups, or as a class. When students are done, discuss the answers for each activity.

Extensions

These extension ideas allow you to reuse or expand upon the activities. Share them with students who complete the activities before other students, or have students do them for additional practice with target vocabulary words.

A Choose one of the vocabulary words and make a diagram or picture to show its meaning.

B After you have chosen the correct answer for each sentence, explain why the wrong answer does not make sense in the sentence.

WORD ROOT

Make sure that students understand that a fossil can be as large as a dinosaur. Ask students to guess what the word *fossilize* means (*to convert into a fossil*).

C Make up a memory device for recalling the meaning of one of the target words.

D Choose two of the target words and write a single sentence that uses them both correctly.

C. Write the vocabulary word that best completes each pair of sentences.

1. Pollution comes to Earth in _____acid rain_____ .
   Burning coal leads to _____acid rain_____ .

2. Dams make _____hydroelectricity_____ .
   One form of power from water is _____hydroelectricity_____ .

3. A canyon with steep walls is a _____gorge_____ .
   It would be hard to climb out of a _____gorge_____ .

4. People who believe in _____Taoism_____ accept change.
   One belief system in China is called _____Taoism_____ .

5. Not giving people their rights is _____repression_____ .
   Not letting people state their opinions is _____repression_____ .

6. Coal and oil are _____fossil fuels_____ .
   Burning _____fossil fuels_____ makes pollution.

7. The _____distribution_____ of China's resources is not equal.
   The spread of things is their _____distribution_____ .

8. The water held back by a dam is a _____reservoir_____ .
   A lake made by people can be used as a _____reservoir_____ .

9. Freedom of speech and religion are two _____human rights_____ .
   China does not always give its citizens _____human rights_____ .

10. A belief system that values family relations is _____Confucianism_____ .
    Respect for the elderly is part of _____Confucianism_____ .

Students' answers will vary.

D. Use each word in a sentence that shows you understand the meaning of the word.

1. Confucianism _Confucianism teaches respect for old people and the value of education._

2. hydroelectricity _The Three Gorges Dam project creates hydroelectricity._

3. human rights _People march and demonstrate in support of human rights in China._

4. distribution _The distribution of China's natural resources is uneven._

5. fossil fuels _Burning fossil fuels, such as coal, causes air pollution._

6. repression _The repression of free speech is a problem in many countries._

7. acid rain _Acid rain brings pollution in the air to the ground._

8. reservoir _Water in a reservoir may be used for drinking or irrigation._

9. Taoism _Taoism teaches people to accept change._

10. gorge _A gorge is a canyon with very steep sides._

Write!

Write your response to the prompt on a separate sheet of paper. Use as many vocabulary words as you can in your writing.

What might be the solutions to some of China's problems?

Write!

Provide each student with a copy of Writing Graphic Organizer: Two-Column Chart, Teacher Guide page 82. Ask students to label the headings "Problems" and "Possible Solutions." Tell students to record facts about problems in the first column and ways to solve the problems in the second column.

Sample Answer

The Three Gorges Dam will create hydroelectricity and help China meet its energy needs. That will cut down acid rain from burning fossil fuels. It will also help people have power who might not have electricity otherwise. China's repression of human rights can be helped by outside countries. But the real changes have to come from within the country. If government leaders believed in and practiced Confucianism and Taoism, China might not have the problems with human rights and pollution that it has.

TAKE-HOME ACTIVITY

Assign the Take-Home Activity to students for additional practice with the target vocabulary words. The reproducible Take-Home Activity for Lesson 14 is on page 97 of the Teacher Guide.

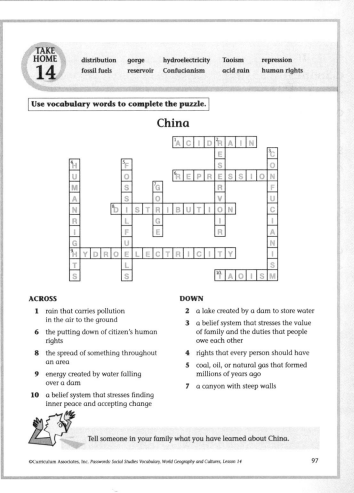

TAKE HOME 14

distribution   gorge   hydroelectricity   Taoism   repression
fossil fuels   reservoir   Confucianism   acid rain   human rights

Use vocabulary words to complete the puzzle.

China

ACROSS

1 rain that carries pollution in the air to the ground
6 the putting down of citizen's human rights
8 the spread of something throughout an area
9 energy created by water falling over a dam
10 a belief system that stresses finding inner peace and accepting change

DOWN

2 a lake created by a dam to store water
3 a belief system that stresses the value of family and the duties that people owe each other
4 rights that every person should have
5 coal, oil, or natural gas that formed millions of years ago
7 a canyon with steep walls

Tell someone in your family what you have learned about China.

©Curriculum Associates, Inc. *Passwords: Social Studies Vocabulary, World Geography and Cultures, Lesson 14*   97

China

LESSON 15

Oceania, Australia, and Antarctica

(Student Book pages 88–93)

TARGET VOCABULARY

atoll a ring-shaped coral island

coral reef an ocean barrier made up of the hard skeletons of billions of coral

lagoon a shallow area of ocean water

species a separate kind of plant or animal

frigid extremely cold

ice cap a thick layer of ice and snow

Aborigines the first people of Australia

outback the flat, dry interior plains of Australia

global warming the rise in the temperature of Earth's lands and oceans

indigenous related to the people, plants, or animals that live naturally in a place

COGNATES

Spanish-speaking students may find a discussion of the similarities and differences between English and Spanish cognates helpful.

English	Spanish
atoll	atolón
lagoon	laguna
species	especie
frigid	frigido
Aborigines	aborígenes
indigenous	indígena

Lesson Summary Coral live in the seas near Australia and Oceania. Some form atolls. Others form coral reefs that are homes to many species. Many species, including humans, cannot live in Antarctica because it is so frigid. Almost all of Antarctica is covered by an ice cap. The people of Australia include the Aborigines. They live in the outback. One challenge in this region is global warming. Global warming is melting the ice cap and killing coral reefs.

BEFORE READING

Activate Prior Knowledge

Write the selection title "Oceania, Australia, and Antarctica" on the board. Under it, write these headings from the reading in a three-column chart: "Special Lands and Creatures;" "Australia's First People;" and "Challenges of Global Warming." Invite students to make a prediction about what is covered under each heading. Then invite them to predict which vocabulary words fall under each heading. Record their predictions. Revisit and discuss their predictions after reading.

Introduce Target Vocabulary

Tell students that they are about to read a selection about Australia, Oceania, and Antarctica. Write the target vocabulary words on the board. Model the pronunciation of each word and have student volunteers repeat the word. Discuss the meaning of each word and, if necessary, write the definition next to the word.

Present Graphic Organizer

Provide each student with a copy of Vocabulary Graphic Organizer: Word Web, Teacher Guide page 79. Have each student choose a target vocabulary word or assign a target word to each student. As students read, they should add information to the graphic organizer.

Word and Definition Cards
for Lesson 15 are on pages 127 and
128 of the Teacher Guide.

VOCABULARY STRATEGY: Print Features

Review with students why a word might appear in boldfaced type in a textbook. *(It is an important new word. It will be defined in the text.)* Tell students that they can often find the meaning of a word in bold type close to where the word appears in the text. Refer students to the first paragraph of the selection.

Ask students what three terms appear in bold (*atoll, coral reef, lagoon*). Then have students find the meanings of the words. Tell students to draw an arrow from each word that appears in bold type to the part of the sentence that gives the meaning of the word.

Oceania, Australia, and Antarctica

atoll   lagoon   frigid   Aborigines   global warming
coral reef   species   ice cap   outback   indigenous

There are thousands of islands in the Pacific Ocean. One is a continent. Others are tiny. Read this selection to learn more about them.

Oceania, Australia, and Antarctica

Special Lands and Creatures

Oceania includes the islands and archipelagos of the Pacific Ocean. Oceania has many small colonies of coral. Coral are small sea creatures. Sometimes, the colonies form an atoll. An **atoll** is a ring-shaped coral island. Atolls are not much above sea level.

In time, many atolls might form a coral reef. A **coral reef** is an ocean barrier. It is made up of the hard skeletons of billions of coral. Such a reef is parallel to the shore. The Great Barrier Reef in Australia is 1,250 miles long! A **lagoon** is a shallow area of ocean water. It is often found between a coral reef and the shore. A lagoon may also be found in the middle of an atoll.

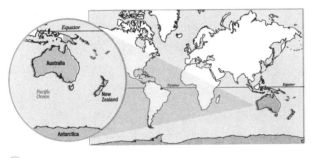

A coral reef is home to many species. A **species** is a separate kind of plant or animal. The Great Barrier Reef has 200 species of birds. It has more than 1,500 species of fish. Australia also has unusual land species. Kangaroos and koala bears are found only in Australia.

Penguins live in Antarctica. People do not. It is **frigid**, or extremely cold. Winds can blow at more than 100 miles per hour. Almost all of Antarctica is covered by an ice cap. An **ice cap** is a thick layer of ice and snow.

Many different species of shark live in the Great Barrier Reef.

Australia's First People

Aborigines, Australia's first people, arrived more than 30,000 years ago. In the late 1700s, Europeans came to Australia. Today, 85 percent of Australians live in cities. Others live in the outback. The **outback** is the dry plains in the center of Australia. People there graze sheep on the sparse grass.

Challenges of Global Warming

Global warming is the rise in the temperature of Earth's lands and oceans. Warmer ocean water is killing coral reefs. It is also melting Antarctica's ice. Melting ice causes oceans to rise. Warmer temperatures are also killing indigenous animals. **Indigenous** means "natural or native to a place." It refers to the people, plants, or animals that arose there.

Climate change affects people too. The world is having extreme weather. Scientists around the world agree. We must work together to stop global warming.

These Aborigines presented a concert of native music in Australia.

My World Geography Vocabulary
Go to page 98 to list other words you have learned about Oceania, Australia, and Antarctica.

DURING READING

Read the selection aloud to students as they follow along in their book, pausing at the end of each paragraph or section. Review any words or concepts that students are having trouble understanding. Remind students that there is a glossary at the back of their book that contains all of the words that appear in boldfaced type in the lesson.

- Draw a Venn diagram to compare and contrast the terms *atoll* and *coral reef*. As students provide ideas, elicit the terms *lagoon, species,* and *global warming*.

- Write the word *Antarctica* at the center of a cluster diagram. Guide students to develop the cluster by describing who or what lives there, what it is like, where it is, and what problems it faces.

- Draw an outline map of Australia. Ask students to identify where, generally, the outback is, and to tell who lives there. Ask whether the term *indigenous* applies to the Aborigines, and why or why not.

- Explain where the coral reef is in relation to Australia. Ask students to identify places where they might find lagoons.

Have students read the selection again on their own.

AFTER READING

Review Graphic Organizer

Answer any questions students have about the reading selection. Then have students complete or review their graphic organizer and share it with the class.

Summarize

Have students work together to come up with either a written or an oral summary of the lesson. Encourage students to use the target vocabulary words as the basis of their summary. Have students share their summary with the class.

My Social Studies Vocabulary

Encourage students to turn to My Social Studies Vocabulary on page 98 of the student book and use the space provided to add other words about Oceania, Australia, and Antarctica.

Oceania, Australia, and Antarctica

A. Match each word with its meaning. Write the letter of the correct meaning on the line in front of each word.

1. __j__ species
2. __e__ ice cap
3. __a__ outback
4. __h__ atoll
5. __c__ global warming
6. __b__ frigid
7. __d__ coral reef
8. __g__ indigenous
9. __f__ Aborigines
10. __i__ lagoon

a. the dry plains in the center of Australia
b. extremely cold
c. the rise in the temperature of Earth's lands and oceans
d. an ocean barrier made up of the hard skeletons of billions of coral
e. a thick layer of ice and snow
f. Australia's first people
g. natural or native to a place
h. a ring-shaped coral island that does not rise much above sea level
i. the shallow ocean water between a coral reef and the shore
j. a separate kind of living thing

B. Choose and write the two words that best complete each sentence.

coral reef   frigid   atoll   ice cap

1. Antarctica is a ____frigid____ continent mostly covered by an ____ice cap____ .

coral reef   indigenous   species   atoll

2. Fish of many different ____species____ live in a ____coral reef____ .

Aborigines   lagoon   outback   global warming

3. The first people to live in Australia's ____outback____ were ____Aborigines____ .

global warming   frigid   Aborigines   indigenous

4. Animals that are ____indigenous____ to Australia and Antarctica are being killed by ____global warming____ .

lagoon   ice cap   atoll   outback

5. A large ____atoll____ might surround a shallow ____lagoon____ .

ROOT
The word **species** has its roots in the Latin word **species**, which means "kind" or "sort."

ACTIVITIES A–D

Encourage students to complete as many of the activities as possible. Remind students that they may refer to the Glossary at the back of their book as they complete the activities. Students may work independently, in small groups, or as a class. When students are done, discuss the answers for each activity.

Extensions

These extension ideas allow you to reuse or expand upon the activities. Share them with students who complete the activities before other students, or have students do them for additional practice with target vocabulary words.

A Look up two of the target vocabulary words in the Glossary, in the dictionary, and in an encyclopedia. How are the definitions similar? How are they different?

B Make a chart with three columns. Label the headings "People or Animals," "Places," and "Things." Write the target vocabulary words in the correct column of the chart. Decide which word does not belong in any of the columns.

WORD ROOT

Write and say these words: *special, specialist,* and *specific.* Ask students how the spellings and meanings of these words are related to the Latin word *species,* meaning "kind" or "sort."

C Draw a diagram showing how any two target vocabulary words are related. For example, you might use a diagram to show how one thing leads to or causes another, or how one or more words fall into a category named by another word or by a place name.

D Choose three target vocabulary words and write a sentence using all three.

atoll   lagoon   frigid   Aborigines   global warming
coral reef   species   ice cap   outback   indigenous

C. *Write the vocabulary word that best completes each pair of sentences.*

1. The first Australians were _____Aborigines_____.

   _____Aborigines_____ know how to survive in the outback.

2. Antarctica is mostly covered by an _____ice cap_____.

   An _____ice cap_____ is made of ice and snow.

3. Animals are being killed by _____global warming_____.

   Many countries want to stop _____global warming_____.

4. Australia's plains are called the _____outback_____.

   Sheep eat the grass on Australia's _____outback_____.

5. Global warming is killing many _____species_____ of plants.

   A coral reef is home to many _____species_____ of fish.

6. The Great Barrier Reef is a _____coral reef_____.

   Billions of coral skeletons make up a _____coral reef_____.

7. A temperature of –94°F would feel _____frigid_____.

   Weather in Antarctica is _____frigid_____.

8. A small coral island is an _____atoll_____.

   An _____atoll_____ is just above sea level.

9. The shore and the reef are separated by a _____lagoon_____.

   An atoll might have a _____lagoon_____ in its center.

10. A kangaroo is _____indigenous_____ to Australia.

    Some of Australia's _____indigenous_____ animal species are seen nowhere else.

92   *Oceania, Australia, and Antarctica*

---

atoll   lagoon   frigid   Aborigines   global warming
coral reef   species   ice cap   outback   indigenous

Students' answers will vary.

D. *Use each pair of words in a sentence.*

1. global warming, ice cap
   Global warming is melting Antarctica's ice cap.

2. frigid, coral reef
   You would see a coral reef in a warm area, not a frigid one.

3. Aborigines, outback
   Many Aborigines still live in the outback.

4. indigenous, species
   Global warming is killing some indigenous species.

5. lagoon, atoll
   An atoll might have a lagoon filled with ocean water.

Write!

Write your response to the prompt on a separate sheet of paper. Use as many vocabulary words as you can in your writing.

Imagine that you could spend a week exploring any place in this region. Where would you go? Why?

Oceania, Australia, and Antarctica   93

Write!

Provide each student with a copy of Writing Graphic Organizer: Topic Web, Teacher Guide page 83. Tell students to write the places they would like to go and things they would like to do or see in each circle. Tell students that they can add more circles to the web if they need to.

Sample Answer

I would go to the Great Barrier Reef. I'd like to swim in a warm lagoon. I'd also like to snorkel around the coral reef. I want to see all the different indigenous species of fish before global warming kills them. I'd like to explore some small atolls too, and maybe look for pirate treasure.

TAKE-HOME ACTIVITY

Assign the Take-Home Activity to students for additional practice with the target vocabulary words. The reproducible Take-Home Activity for Lesson 15 is on page 98 of the Teacher Guide.

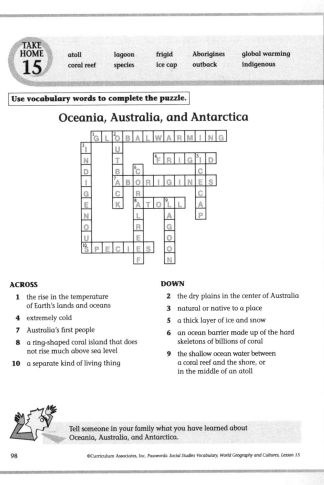

TAKE HOME 15

atoll   lagoon   frigid   Aborigines   global warming
coral reef   species   ice cap   outback   indigenous

Use vocabulary words to complete the puzzle.

Oceania, Australia, and Antarctica

ACROSS
1 the rise in the temperature of Earth's lands and oceans
4 extremely cold
7 Australia's first people
8 a ring-shaped coral island that does not rise much above sea level
10 a separate kind of living thing

DOWN
2 the dry plains in the center of Australia
3 natural or native to a place
5 a thick layer of ice and snow
6 an ocean barrier made up of the hard skeletons of billions of coral
9 the shallow ocean water between a coral reef and the shore, or in the middle of an atoll

Tell someone in your family what you have learned about Oceania, Australia, and Antarctica.

98   ©Curriculum Associates, Inc. *Passwords: Social Studies Vocabulary, World Geography and Cultures, Lesson 15*

Oceania, Australia, and Antarctica   **75**

Vocabulary Graphic Organizer: Word Wheel

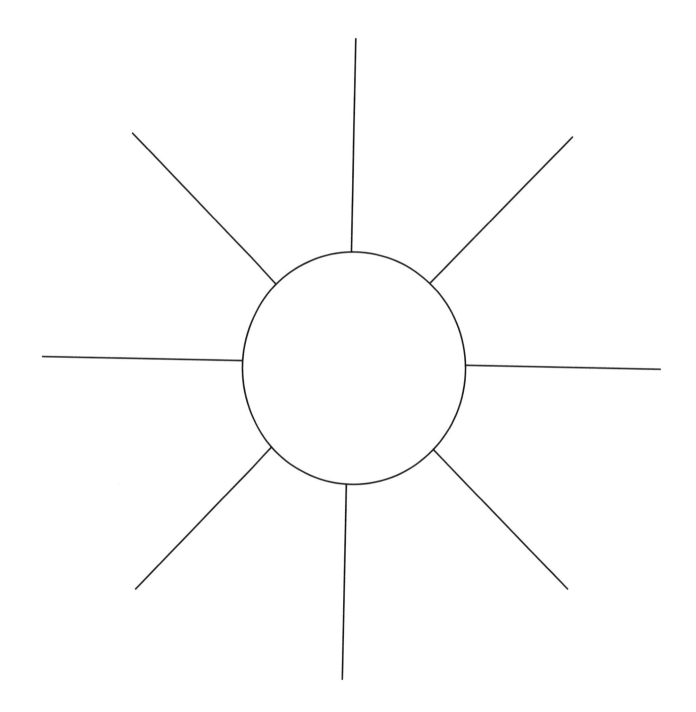

©Curriculum Associates, Inc. *Passwords: Social Studies Vocabulary, World Geography and Cultures*

Name _____ Date _____

Vocabulary Graphic Organizer: What Is It Like?

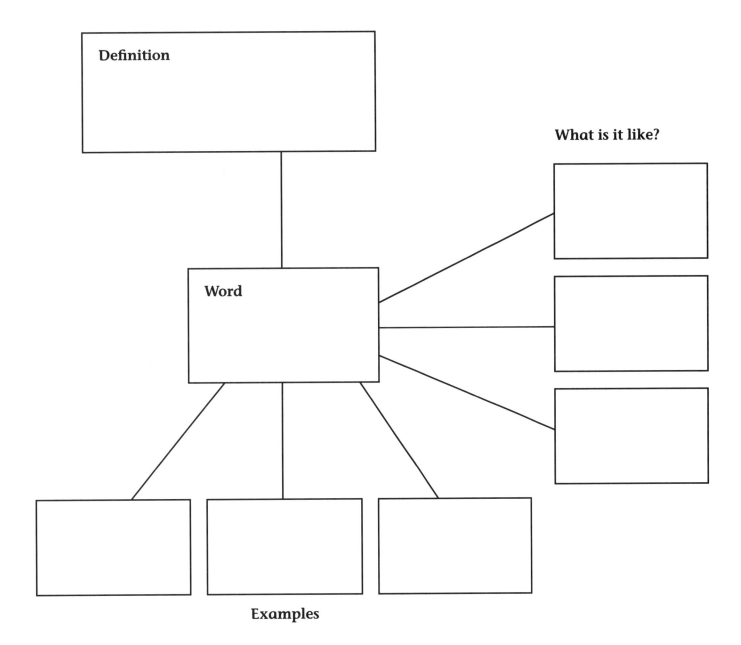

Definition

Word

What is it like?

Examples

Vocabulary Graphic Organizer: Vocabulary Map

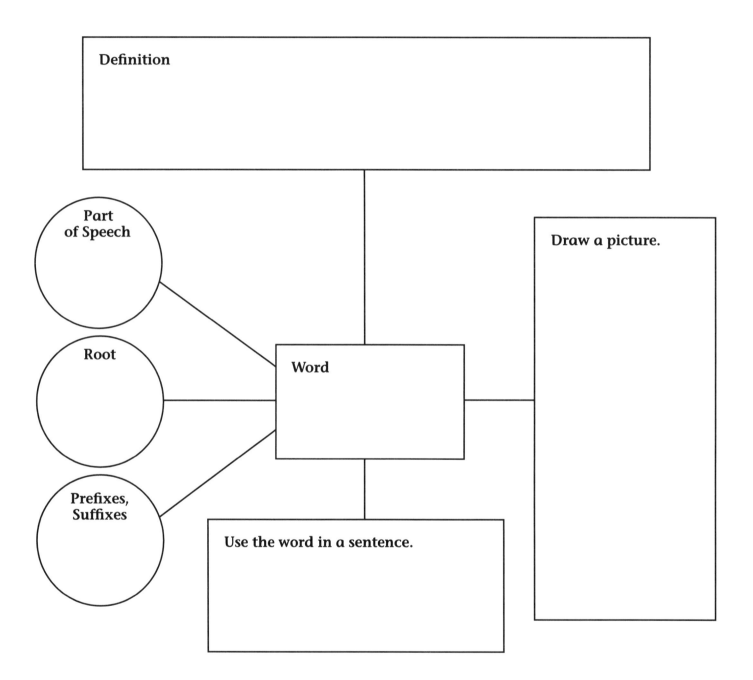

Definition

Part of Speech

Root

Prefixes, Suffixes

Word

Draw a picture.

Use the word in a sentence.

Vocabulary Graphic Organizer: Word Web

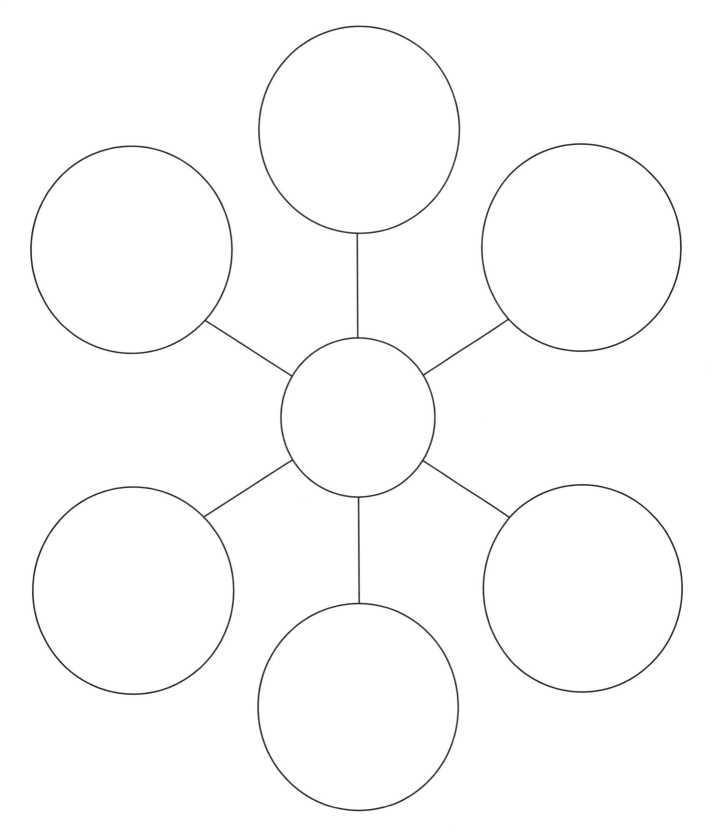

Name _____ Date _____

Writing Graphic Organizer: Cause and Effect Chart

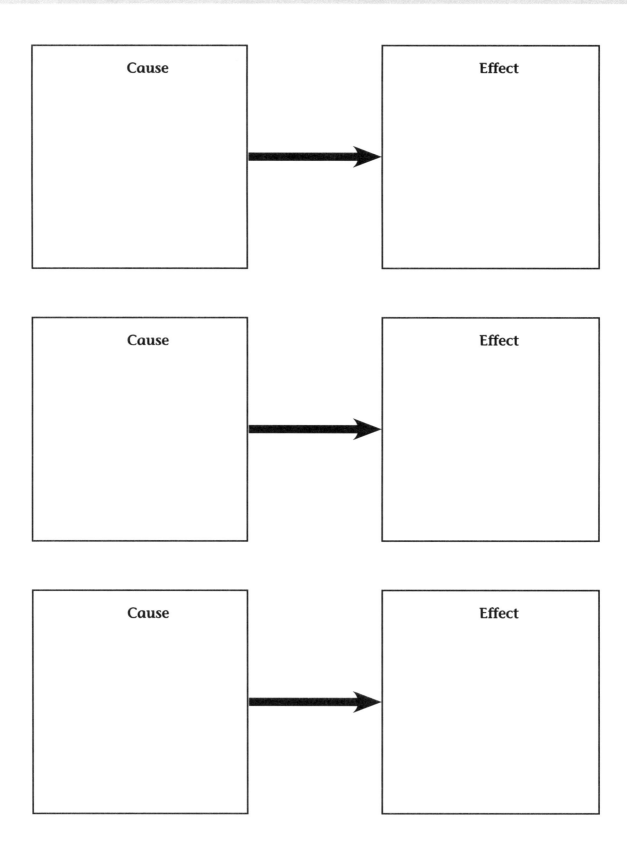

Writing Graphic Organizer: Main Idea and Details Chart

Main Idea	Details
1.	
2.	
3.	

Writing Graphic Organizer: Two-Column Chart

Writing Graphic Organizer: Topic Web

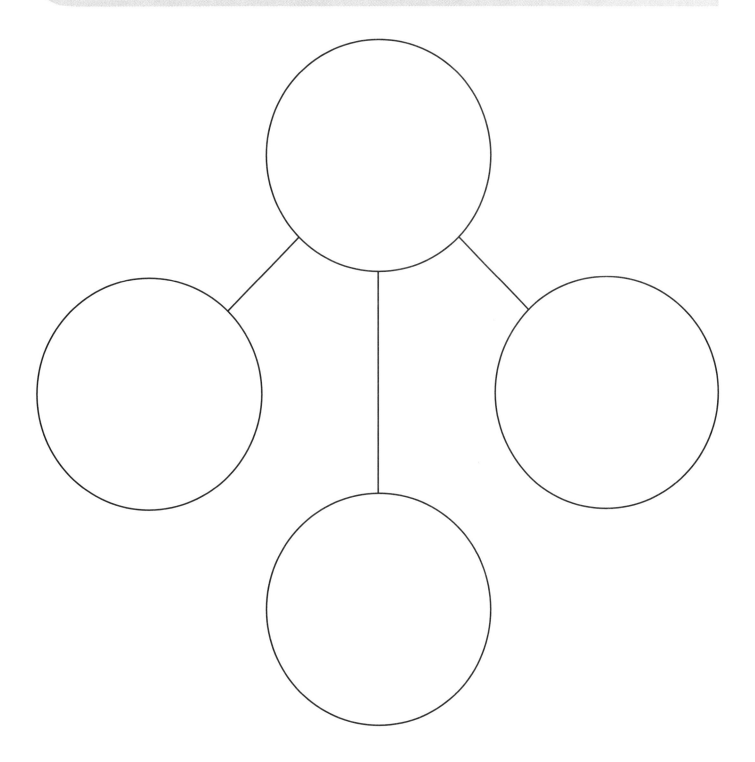

TAKE
HOME
1

| geography | climate | agriculture | delta | civilization |
| landform | vegetation | fertile | river system | irrigation |

Use vocabulary words to complete the puzzle.

Geography—Looking at the World

ACROSS

5 plant life, including trees, bushes, and grasses

7 the study of the earth and the relationship between people and the earth

8 low, watery land formed by a fan-shaped system of streams near the mouth of a river

9 bringing water to dry land

10 the weather in an area over a period of time

DOWN

1 able to produce many crops

2 a network of streams and rivers that feed into a main river

3 a large, organized group of people

4 the growing of crops

6 a feature of Earth's surface

Tell someone in your family what you have learned about geography— looking at the world.

continent   hemisphere   longitude   absolute location   map key

equator   latitude   degree   relative location   map scale

Use vocabulary words to complete the puzzle.

The Tools of Geography

ACROSS

4 a comparison between the distance shown on a map and actual distances on Earth

6 one of Earth's seven major landmasses

7 the unit of measure of latitude and longitude

8 the position of one place in relation to another place

9 a place's exact location on a grid of latitude and longitude

DOWN

1 an imaginary line around the middle of Earth

2 a series of imaginary lines that circle Earth from east to west

3 a series of imaginary lines that run from the North Pole to the South Pole

4 tells what the lines, colors, and symbols on a map mean

5 half of Earth

Tell someone in your family what you have learned about the tools of geography.

culture   economy   urban   population density

culture region   migration   industrialization   cultural diversity

government   rural

Use vocabulary words to complete the puzzle.

World Cultures

ACROSS

2 a system in which people sell or trade goods and services

4 a small group of people who make laws and rule a large group of people

7 a way of life of a group of people

8 the making of many goods by machine

9 having people from a variety of cultures

10 the average number of people per square mile living in an area

DOWN

1 a city area

3 an area where many people share the same culture

5 an area having many open spaces and few people

6 the movement of people from one place to another

Tell someone in your family what you have learned about world cultures.

natural resource   plain   capitalism   technology

mountain range   standard of living   market economy   free trade

tributary   immigrant

Use vocabulary words to complete the puzzle.

The United States and Canada

ACROSS

1 a long chain of mountains

4 an economic system in which private owners control and use resources for profit

7 something in nature that people can use

8 the use of new ideas and machines to improve people's lives

9 a measure of the quality of life

DOWN

1 when business owners compete with one another to sell goods and services

2 a stream that joins others and flows into a river or lake

3 someone who comes to a country to live

5 a flat land with few trees

6 the selling of goods from one country to another without taxes

Tell someone in your family what you have learned about the United States and Canada.

volcano   tropical climate   developing country   export
elevation   colonization   cash crop   deforestation
plateau   descendant

Use vocabulary words to complete the puzzle.

Latin America

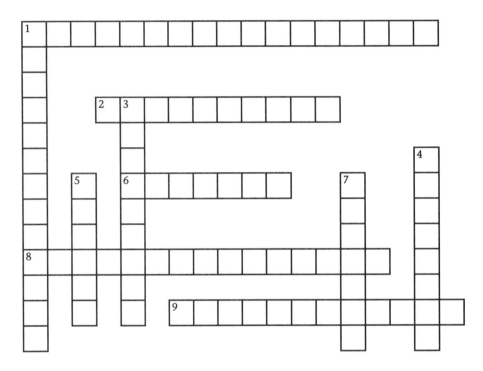

ACROSS

1 a country that is moving from an economy based on farming to one based on industry

2 someone related to an earlier person or group

6 an opening in Earth's crust through which rock and gases flow

8 weather that is always very warm and moist

9 the making of settlements in another land

DOWN

1 the cutting down of a forest

3 height, as in a mountain

4 a crop that is raised to sell

5 a good that is sold to another country

7 a high, flat landform

Tell someone in your family what you have learned about Latin America.

TAKE HOME 6

peninsula   ethnic conflict   service industry   European Union
channel   border   tourism   common currency
ethnic group   manufacturing

Use vocabulary words to complete the puzzle.

Europe

ACROSS

1 a system of money that is shared by different countries

7 a group of people who have common ancestors, history, language, and way of life

8 an area of land that extends from a landmass and is mostly surrounded by water

9 a group of businesses that provide services

10 fighting among ethnic groups

DOWN

2 the making of goods by machine

3 a narrow sea between two large areas of land

4 a group of countries in Europe that are working together to make better lives for their people

5 the business of helping people travel on vacations

6 an imaginary line that separates countries

Tell someone in your family what you have learned about Europe.

tundra   steppe   collective farm   consumer good

permafrost   communism   privatization   pollution

taiga   command economy

Use vocabulary words to complete the puzzle.

Russia

ACROSS

4   a farm that the Soviet government owned and managed

5   a dry, flat grassland

7   a flat, bare plain with no trees

9   the poisoning of water, land, and air

10   an economy in which the government decides what to produce

DOWN

1   a product that people use

2   ground that is always frozen

3   the process of replacing government ownership of businesses with private ownership

6   an economic system in which the government owns all property and businesses

8   an area of evergreen forests

Tell someone in your family what you have learned about Russia.

TAKE HOME 8

desert   overgrazing   nationalism   mosque   petroleum
oasis   arable   Islam   theocracy supply and demand

Use vocabulary words to complete the puzzle.

North Africa and Southwest Asia

ACROSS

3 a Muslim building of worship

7 suitable for use as farmland

8 a religion based on the teachings of Muhammad

9 a sandy or rocky area with little or no rainfall

10 an economic concept that states that the price of a good rises or falls depending on how many people want it and on how much of the good is available

DOWN

1 an oily liquid that people burn to create energy

2 a strong pride in and loyalty to one's country

4 what happens when animals eat grass faster than it can grow back

5 a government ruled by a religious leader

6 an area in a desert that has water underground

Tell someone in your family what you have learned about North Africa and Southwest Asia.

drought   rift   overpopulation   life expectancy
savanna   subsistence farming   famine   clan
endangered   illiterate

Use vocabulary words to complete the puzzle.

Africa South of the Sahara

ACROSS

2 growing only enough crops to provide for one's basic food needs

5 flat grassland with a few trees and shrubs

7 a long time without rain

8 how long people are expected to live

10 having more people in an area than the resources can support

DOWN

1 a broad, steep-walled valley

3 unable to read and write

4 close to disappearing forever because there are so few

6 a serious food shortage that causes people to die

9 a group of people who are related

Tell someone in your family what you have learned about Africa South of the Sahara.

landlocked   precipitation   earthquake   nomad   Silk Road
arid   erosion   tribe   tradition   emigrate

Use vocabulary words to complete the puzzle.

Central Asia

ACROSS

1 water that falls to Earth as rain or snow

4 to leave a country in order to live in another

6 surrounded by land

9 a belief or custom handed down from one generation to the next

10 a trade route that went from China, through Central Asia, to the Mediterranean Sea

DOWN

2 the wearing away of land

3 a group of people who share a way of life

5 a shaking of part of Earth's surface

7 dry

8 a person who travels from place to place

Tell someone in your family what you have learned about Central Asia.

TAKE HOME 11

subcontinent	Hinduism	Buddhism	Green Revolution
monsoon	reincarnation	pagoda	information technology
dialect	caste		

Use vocabulary words to complete the puzzle.

South Asia

ACROSS

2 a movement aimed at improving farming methods and crop yields

5 a tower built on many levels

8 a large area that is cut off from the rest of a continent by land features

9 a religion that believes in many gods and reincarnation

10 the use of computer hardware, software, and the Internet to help people to process information

DOWN

1 the idea that each soul must be reborn many times

3 a social group into which a person is born and cannot change

4 a seasonal wind that changes direction twice a year

6 a different form of the same language

7 a religion that began in India that teaches that people are too attached to the things of this world

Tell someone in your family what you have learned about South Asia.

94   ©Curriculum Associates, Inc. *Passwords: Social Studies Vocabulary, World Geography and Cultures, Lesson 11*

archipelago   Ring of Fire   typhoon   paddy   port
inhabited   tsunami   cultivation terrace farming strait

Use vocabulary words to complete the puzzle.

Southeast Asia

ACROSS

2 the act of preparing land and growing crops

6 an area of volcanic activity along the Pacific Ocean

7 a group of islands

9 the growing of crops on step-like levels cut into the soil

10 a flooded field where rice is grown

DOWN

1 a place where ships can dock

3 a violent storm that occurs in the Pacific Ocean

4 a narrow strip of water between large areas of land

5 having people living in a place

8 a huge sea wave caused by an underwater earthquake

Tell someone in your family what you have learned about Southeast Asia.

Use vocabulary words to complete the puzzle.

East Asia

ACROSS

1 the state of relying on and affecting many others

7 a form of Japanese drama that combines singing, dancing, bold makeup, and elaborate costumes

8 cut off from other areas and people

9 more exports than imports

10 a society made up of mostly the same kind of people

DOWN

2 more imports than exports

3 the art of beautiful writing

4 an economy that is international

5 forms of fighting and exercise that use the hands and feet

6 a traditional Japanese poem

Tell someone in your family what you have learned about East Asia.

©Curriculum Associates, Inc. *Passwords: Social Studies Vocabulary, World Geography and Cultures, Lesson 13*

distribution   gorge   hydroelectricity   Taoism   repression
fossil fuels   reservoir   Confucianism   acid rain   human rights

Use vocabulary words to complete the puzzle.

China

ACROSS

1 rain that carries pollution
   in the air to the ground

6 the putting down of citizen's human
   rights

8 the spread of something throughout
   an area

9 energy created by water falling
   over a dam

10 a belief system that stresses finding
   inner peace and accepting change

DOWN

2 a lake created by a dam to store water

3 a belief system that stresses the value
   of family and the duties that people
   owe each other

4 rights that every person should have

5 coal, oil, or natural gas that formed
   millions of years ago

7 a canyon with steep walls

Tell someone in your family what you have learned about China.

TAKE HOME 15

| atoll | lagoon | frigid | Aborigines | global warming |
| coral reef | species | ice cap | outback | indigenous |

Use vocabulary words to complete the puzzle.

Oceania, Australia, and Antarctica

ACROSS

1 the rise in the temperature of Earth's lands and oceans

4 extremely cold

7 Australia's first people

8 a ring-shaped coral island that does not rise much above sea level

10 a separate kind of living thing

DOWN

2 the dry plains in the center of Australia

3 natural or native to a place

5 a thick layer of ice and snow

6 an ocean barrier made up of the hard skeletons of billions of coral

9 the shallow ocean water between a coral reef and the shore, or in the middle of an atoll

Tell someone in your family what you have learned about Oceania, Australia, and Antarctica.

©Curriculum Associates, Inc. *Passwords: Social Studies Vocabulary, World Geography and Cultures, Lesson 15*

geography	fertile
landform	delta
climate	river system
vegetation	civilization
agriculture	irrigation

able to produce many crops

the study of Earth's surface, weather, and the living things on it

a low, watery land formed by a fan-shaped system of streams near the mouth of a river

a feature of Earth's surface

a network of streams and rivers that feeds into a main river

the weather in an area over a period of time

a large, organized group of people

plant life, including trees, bushes, and grasses

the process of bringing water to dry land

the growing of crops

continent	degree
equator	absolute location
hemisphere	relative location
latitude	map key
longitude	map scale

the unit of measure of latitude and longitude, one 360th distance around Earth

one of Earth's seven major landmasses

a place's exact location on a grid of latitude and longitude

an imaginary line around the middle of Earth

the position of one place in relation to another place

half of Earth

a guide to the lines, colors, and symbols on a map

a series of imaginary lines that circle Earth from east to west

a comparison between distances shown on a map to actual distances on Earth

a series of imaginary lines that run from the North Pole to the South Pole

culture	rural
culture region	urban
government	industrialization
economy	population density
migration	cultural diversity

an area having many open spaces and few people

the way of life of a group of people

related to the city

an area where many people share the same culture

the making of many goods by machine

a small group of people who make laws and rule a large group of people

the average number of people per square mile living in an area

a system in which people sell or trade goods and services

having people from a variety of cultures

the movement of people from one place to another

natural resource	standard of living
mountain range	capitalism
tributary	market economy
plain	technology
immigrant	free trade

a measure of the quality of life; includes having good food, housing, education, and healthcare

something in nature that people can use

an economic system in which private owners control and use resources for profit

a long chain of mountains

a system in which business owners compete with one another to sell goods and services

a stream that joins others and flows into a river or lake

a way of using new ideas and machines to improve people's lives

a flat land with few trees, also called a prairie

the selling of goods from one country to another without taxes

someone who comes to another country to live

volcano	descendant
elevation	developing country
plateau	cash crop
tropical climate	export
colonization	deforestation

someone related to an earlier person or group

an opening in Earth's crust through which rock and gases flow

a country that is moving from an economy based on farming to one based on industry

height, as in the measure of a mountain

a crop that is raised to sell

a high, flat landform

a good that is sold to another country

weather that is always very warm and moist

the cutting down of forests

the setting up of settlements in another land

peninsula	manufacturing
channel	service industry
ethnic group	tourism
ethnic conflict	European Union
border	common currency

the making of goods by machine

an area of land that extends from a landmass and is mostly surrounded by water

a group of businesses that provide services

a narrow sea between two large areas of land

the business of helping people travel on vacations

a group of people who have common ancestors, history, language, and way of life

a group of countries in Europe that are working together to make better lives for their people

fighting among ethnic groups

a system of money that is shared by different countries

an imaginary line that separates countries

tundra	command economy
permafrost	collective farm
taiga	privatization
steppe	consumer good
communism	pollution

an economy in which the government decides what goods to produce, not the people or business owners	a flat, bare plain with no trees
a farm that the Soviet government owned and managed	an area where the ground is always frozen a little below the surface
the process of replacing government ownership of businesses with private ownership	an area of evergreen forests
a product that people use	a dry, flat grassland
the poisoning of water, land, and air	an economic system in which the government owns all property and businesses

desert

Islam

oasis

mosque

overgrazing

theocracy

arable

petroleum

nationalism

supply and
demand

a religion based on the teachings
of Muhammad

a sandy or rocky area with little
or no rainfall

a Muslim building of worship

an area in the desert that has water
from underground

a government ruled by
a religious leader

what happens when animals eat
grass faster than it can grow back

an oily liquid that people burn to
create energy

land suitable for use as farmland

an economic concept that states
that the price of a good rises or falls
depending on how many people
want it and on how much
of the good is available

a strong pride in and loyalty
to one's country

©Curriculum Associates, Inc. *Passwords: Social Studies Vocabulary, World Geography and Cultures, Lesson 8—Word Cards*

drought	illiterate
savanna	overpopulation
endangered	famine
rift	life expectancy
subsistence farming	clan

unable to read and write	a long time without rain
having more people in an area than the resources can support	flat grassland with a few trees and shrubs
a serious food shortage that causes people to die	close to disappearing forever because there are so few
how long people are expected to live	a broad, steep-walled valley
a group of people who are related	growing only enough crops to provide for one's basic food needs

landlocked	tribe
arid	nomad
precipitation	tradition
erosion	Silk Road
earthquake	emigrate

a group of people who share
a way of life

surrounded by land

a person who travels from place
to place in search of food
or grazing for animals

dry

a belief or custom handed down
from one generation to the next

water that falls to Earth as rain
or snow

a trade route that went from China,
through Central Asia, to the
Mediterranean Sea

the wearing away of land by water,
wind, or ice

to leave a country in order to live
in another

a shaking of part of Earth's surface
as a result of underground forces

©Curriculum Associates, Inc. *Passwords: Social Studies Vocabulary, World Geography and Cultures, Lesson 10—Word Cards*

subcontinent	caste
monsoon	Buddhism
dialect	pagoda
Hinduism	Green Revolution
reincarnation	information technology

a social group one is born into and cannot change

a large area that is cut off from the rest of a continent by land features

the religion that began in India that teaches that people are too attached to the things of this world

a seasonal wind that changes direction twice a year

an Asian tower with many levels that may serve as a temple

a different version of the same language

a movement aimed to improve farming methods and crop yields

an Indian religion based on the belief in many gods and reincarnation

the use of computer hardware, software, and the Internet to help people to process information

the idea that each soul must be reborn many times

archipelago

cultivation

inhabited

paddy

Ring of Fire

terrace farming

tsunami

port

typhoon

strait

the act of preparing land and growing crops	a group of many islands
a flooded field where rice is grown	having people living there
the growing of crops on step-like levels cut into the soil	an area of volcanic activity along the Pacific Ocean
a place where ships can dock	a huge sea wave caused by an underwater earthquake
a narrow strip of water between large areas of land	a violent storm that occurs in the Pacific Ocean

isolation

martial arts

homogeneous
society

global
economy

haiku

interdependence

calligraphy

trade surplus

kabuki

trade deficit

forms of fighting and exercise that use the hands and feet

a state of being cut off from other areas and people

a world economic system

a society made up of mostly the same kind of people

the state of countries relying on and affecting each other

a traditional Japanese poem written in three lines with five, seven, and five syllables

the result of more exports than imports

the art of beautiful writing

the result of more imports than exports

a form of Japanese drama that combines singing, dancing, bold makeup, and elaborate costumes

distribution	Confucianism
fossil fuels	Taoism
gorge	acid rain
reservoir	repression
hydroelectricity	human rights

a belief system that stresses the value of family and the duties that people owe each other

the spread of something

a belief system that stresses finding inner peace and accepting change

coal, oil, or natural gas that formed millions of years ago

rain that carries pollution in the air to the ground

a canyon with steep walls

the putting down of something, such as citizens' human rights

a lake created to store water

rights that every person should have

energy created by water falling over a dam

atoll

ice cap

coral reef

Aborigines

lagoon

outback

species

global
warming

frigid

indigenous

a thick layer of ice and snow

a ring-shaped coral island that does not rise much above sea level

Australia's first people

an ocean barrier made up of the hard skeletons of billions of coral

the dry plains in the center of Australia

the shallow ocean water between a coral reef and the shore, or in the middle of an atoll

the rise in the temperature of Earth's lands and oceans

a separate kind of plant or animal

natural, or native to a place

extremely cold